INTRODUCTION.

IN these days of rush and hurry, when in life's race the pace is merry from the jump some at least of the veterans, who are beginning to feel the pinch, may find it agreeable to take a pull at themselves and give a glance back at the country they have crossed and the varied incidents they have met with on the way. And of all the memories of old which may throng back to nerve the fibre or quicken the pulse beat can there be any dearer to the heart of the true sportsman than those associated with the deeds of the thoroughbred ?

"Ah, for the good old times !" sighs the "aged," as his thoughts go back to the days when Banker was a name to conjure with and Archer's triumphs were familiar in the mouth as household words. And who of the later generation will deny that those times were good ? Then, when Victoria was but in the chrysalis state of what we call civilization, there came to her shores much of the finest manhood the Old World ever produced—the bone, the thews, and the brain which lay the foundations of nations. And with them came that great love for sport so specially inherent in the Anglo-Saxon race. Soon the passion took form and illustration—crude and raw, perhaps ; but the process had begun, and time and circumstance were alone required for its full development. So it was but fitting and proper that to aid them in working upward and onward those pioneers should seek to mingle in this southern world some of the best strains of blood which had ever reddened rowel at Doncaster or Epsom. Not only pluck and enthusiasm, but great judgment was required to bring about all these results. Any piece of velvety turf had served in the first days of settlement for a gallop, but as the sport began to grow the necessity of providing it with a proper home became all evident, and what more suitable for a trysting place could have been found the wide world over than that expanse of turf (bordered by the Saltwater River, and emphasised by its natural hill) now known as Flemington. The men who chose that spot as the future chief arena of Australasian racing had not only sound hearts, but clear heads, and time has more than justified their selection. And though the going might not have proved as elastic or tender to Archer's or Banker's hoofs as that which gives emphasis to the stride of a Carbine or Abercorn, still nature could hardly have served the sporting spirit better had she been especially invoked to design a galloping ground. Whatever addition or improvement followed in the process of evolution, took rather the shape of general ornamentation, attraction or convenience now illustrated by the capacious grand stand, the artificially topped hill, the velvet, flower-fringed lawn, and the other surroundings which invite all sorts and conditions of people to the great annual racing carnival of the southern world. But Mr. R. C. Bagot, the chief of the genii, who wrought much of this change for the benefit and comfort of the ever-increasing thousands who thronged yearly to the spot, did not do his work with the rapidity of the Arabian Nights favourites. It was the outcome of much time and travail ; but ere his hand fell powerless he had laid a good foundation for his successor, Mr. Byron Moore, to labour upon. That gentleman seems to have caught the true spirit of the originator's design, and his work promises to even more than fulfil the ambitious hopes and aspirations of him who has left an indelible mark on the records of Australasian racing.

And there are other men who have wrought well and wisely, too, perhaps, in different ways, yet all to the same end. Though many of them have passed away, their memories are kept green, and their names will be remembered as long as the thoroughbred holds a place in the Australian sportsman's heart. Then, again, there are other pioneers—equine pioneers, whose deeds should fittingly serve to preface the records of the Australian turf. The horses were worthy of the times. Both were in the rough, but the quality was there. It only wanted the working up and the time and attention requisite for the proper development of the blood, bone and muscle. And that development has surely been wrought by judicious breeding, careful training, and the constant commingling of fresh strains of blood, combining the Panic stoutness, the Fisherman brilliancy, and the

Musket speed and stamina.   Yet to many of our sportsmen it must seem but as yesterday since The Flying Buck galloped away from his field, on the first Champion Day ; and although twenty-eight spring times have come and gone since the first Melbourne Cup was won and lost, there are doubtless many veterans who in their mind's eye can see Mr. De Mestre's big bay horse, Archer, romping home in front of Mormon and Prince. How he repeated that performance the following year, is a record yet unique in the annals of Victorian racing.   Then the colours of Banker and Lantern flash on the mental eye, and once again we see game old Panic struggling vainly up the straight with his 10st. after little grey Toryboy.   Who that saw the finish between The Barb and Exile will ever forget it.   How the Sydney folk chuckled when Tim Whiffler showed the way to Queen of Hearts, and what long faces Tim's backers wore the following spring, when Glencoe comfortably carried his 9st 11b home in front of old Strop and the grey mare, Shenandoah !   The tales of the heroes of later days need no repetition here.   There still are thousands and tens of thousands of witnesses who can recall to mind the gallant Horatio's vain pursuit of the "cart horse," Don Juan ; of the finish of the three-legged Zulu, and that brilliant rush of Malua's which snatched the victory from old Commotion almost on the post.   The thousands and the tens of thousands can also testify to the flash of the magpie jacket as O'Brien called on Mentor at the distance, and those witnesses will again be able to tell their own stories, in ever increasing volume, of the struggles of future equine heroes up the straight.   They will come as they have come in ever swelling streams since Archer earned his great double event honours, from every quarter of the southern hemisphere : from the back blocks of Queensland, from the pearl fisheries of Western Australia, from the rude grandeurs of New Zealand.

They will come from Collingwood in van, spring cart and lorry ; from Toorak and St. Kilda in barouche, landau and drag.   They will come from all ranks of labour, all grades of humanity ; from the political heads of Government to the budding orators of the debating clubs ; from the wool and quartz king to the shearer and miner ; from the merchant to the storeman ; from the manufacturing magnate to the junior apprentice ; and from the mammoth metallician who deals in "thous." to the aspirant for magic circle honours who rakes in his shilling in his double event book on Collingwood Flat. All these multifarious atoms of sporting and semi-sporting humanity will be attracted again and again, year by year, to Flemington as the great centre of gravity of the Australasian sporting world.   Its gatherings will serve as bright illustrations of the true federation of the Australian colonies.   Legislative sages or political trimmers may seek to foster or mar by their handicraft the growth of a national unity between peoples separated by imaginary boundaries ; but whatever ill or good feelings their efforts may engender, they will never be able to injuriously affect that great federal spirit promoted by the rivalry of the thoroughbred on Flemington turf.   What can more eloquently speak than such reunions of our true kinship, not only with our brothers of the other colonies, but with the parent stock, from which has sprung the bone and gristle of the land ?   Not only with the men, but with the horses.   All trace back to the grand old stud books, with the strains of blood which flowed so freely in that gallop on the Russian guns at Balaclava, which have given glory to the Quorn and the Cotswold, to Assheton Smith, Tom Moody and Whyte Melville in the old pastures, and to the Melbourne and Ballarat "beauties," to Sam Waldock, Lindsay Gordon and George Watson in the new land.   Flying Childers or Ormonde might in a sense have tried conclusions with Banker, Archer or Carbine at Epsom, Doncaster or Flemington.   All the many strains but flow from the one great source.   And in the future, whatever political changes may or may not ensue, there must always remain one great and natural federation—the federation of blood, bone and sinew.

List of Plates.

A. 36029

Index.

M'COMAS
Patent Prize Waterlifters,
Factory—507 COLLINS STREET, MELBOURNE.

Factory—Morts Dock & Engineering Co., Balmain, Sydney.

GENERAL AGENTS—
M'COMAS & CO., 507 COLLINS STREET, MELBOURNE.

Agencies throughout the Colonies and in Calcutta and Bombay.

Over One Hundred Gold, Silver and Bronze Medals. First Prizes and Honors from 1871 to 1889, for Wool-washing, Stock Watering, Irrigation and Station use.

First Prize Special over all exhibits for General Excellence and Value at Sydney International and Adelaide Centennial Exhibition.

Size.	Power and Height.	Quantity per Minute.	Price, with Frame for 12 feet.	Price per foot extra.	Price of 17 feet, complete with Horse-works.	PORTABLE
¾	One man, 35 ft.	30 gallons	£16	10/-	...	...
2½	One man, 15 ft.	60 ,,	£16	10/-	...	...
3½	Two men, 12 ft.	120 ,,	£24, £27	15/-	...	...
5	One horse, 20 ft.	300 ,,	£36	20/-	£85	£130
7	One horse, 8 ft.	1000 ,,	£54	30/-	£100	£150
9	Two horse, 8ft.	2000 ,,	£81	60/-	£120	£200

WATERMAN'S ARMS HOTEL,

LITTLE COLLINS STREET WEST

(Next Jas. M'Ewan and Co.),

TUTTON & SMERDON, PROPRIETORS.

GEORGE TUTTON

Is Registered by Bowes' Tattersall's, V.R.C. and all principal Clubs in Australia, is always seen in the Paddock backing the field, odds from a Sov. to a Hundred.

WOOL.

YOUNGHUSBAND & CO., LTD.,

BROKERS IN

WOOL,
  Sheepskins,
    Hides,
      Tallow,
        Furred Skins,
          Bark,
            And Grain.

SELLING BROKERS ONLY.

Every Consignment meets with Personal Supervision.

————:o:————

Account Sales Promptly Rendered.

Cash advances against Consignments.

AUCTION SALES HELD DAILY.

666 BOURKE STREET,

MELBOURNE.

A CUP RETROSPECT AND PROSPECT.

A SCORE and eight years have passed o'er us.
  They seem like a shadow gone by,
Since **Archer** the great flashed before us
  And won the first Cup—With a sigh
We saw him depart with the second,
  We watched his most marvellous stride,
And none who e'er saw him but reckoned
  A racehorse was wrapped in his hide.

And then came the third, won by **Banker**,
  The fourth by a **Lantern** was lit,
A game little horse ! what a spanker
  He led them whene'er he was fit.
Old **Toryboy's** year was the next one,
  The next the **Black Demon** appeared,
Tim's followed—and then—oh, it vexed one
  To see how our sportsmen were scared.

When Tait made his mind up to win it,
  And did so with gallant **Glencoe**,
Not one of them claimed to be in it,
  Nor e'en had the ghost of a show.
Then **Warrior** (another South Waler)
  Continued to keep up the funk,
And pale grew their lips and still paler,
  When he ran home in front of the Monk.

The tenth showed Tasmania victorious,
  The time was the shortest yet known ;
The finish was something most glorious,
  By Lapdog and **Nimblefoot** shown.
Then followed **The Pearl** and **The Quack**,
  both
  Horses of Honest John Tait's,
Which fact caused the public to back both,
  And win. In the next race the fates

Look'd on Thompson's **Don Juan** most
  kindly,
  And Joe built a mansion of state
With cash which the public most blindly
  Contributed. Such is the fate
Of backers and bookmakers yearly,
  When a flyer is kept very dark ;
The mugs who back doubles pay dearly,
  The winners enjoying the lark.

The next year saw **Haricot** spieling
  Away, well in front of the ruck,
And Chirnside was charmed, no doubt, feeling
  Quite pleased at the change in his luck.
When **Wollomai** walked in a winner,
  To Cleeland's great joy and delight,
The genial John, if a sinner,
  Was highly exalted that night.

See how the bright beauty, **Briseis**,
  Brings Wilson again to the fore ;
No man more delighted than he is
  To win the grand trophy once more.
Charge, **Chester** ! do battle for Sydney,
  And carry the Cup there again ;
We need a few sires of your kidney,
  With pedigree pure, without stain.

And now **Calamia** comes over ;
  So calmly he puts in his claim,
At once puts De Mestre in clover,
  By winning first prize in the game.
The fame of the horse had been sounded
  Which next was to win the great race,
And **Darriwell's** fame was well grounded,
  For time showed how fast was the pace.

This brings **Grand Flaneur** on the scene
  where
  His long list of vict'ries were won ;
A more brilliant horse was ne'er seen there
  Than Yattendon's game, gallant son.
A cripple careered to first place when
  Black **Zulu** from Sydney appeared ;
Five ten brought him home in the race, then
  How loudly the bookmakers cheered.

The **Assyrian** ran home through the rain, in
  Three forty, with seven thirteen ;
The ring laughs and chuckles again, in
  The fact that an outsider's seen
Through the storm, splashing mud in the
  faces
  Of fav'rites, and heavy weights, too,
Whose owners are making grimaces,
  And looking uncommonly blue.

Then **Martini Henri** brought trouble
  On those who had coupled his name
And laid 'gainst him winning the double,
  Which added again to his fame.
The Derby and Cup have been won by
  One horse in the days that have fled,
And Lantern, in days long since gone by,
  His colours to victory led.

While Wilson's Briseis, White's Chester,
  And Long's Grand Flaneur did the same
As Martini Henri—the rest here
  I've mentioned are unknown to fame
So far as a double's concerned ; but
  I've wandered away from my task,
And hasten to tell all I've learned, but
  Your patience I'll venture to ask,

While I tell how **Malua** ran first, in
  The year of one eight eighty four,
When Inglis was cheered with a burst, in
  Which thousands all joined, till a roar
Rose from lawn and from flat, and the air
  with
  Hurrahs, cheers and shouting was full.
And now I would beg you to bear with

Me just while I take a slight pull
On the rein of my fancy, for fear that
  She'll run rather wide of the truth ;
Although I hope not to go near that,
  'Tis needful to travel, forsooth.
Sheet Anchor and Martin are waiting,
  Both owner and horse in their prime,
And truly the field gets a slating,
  Nor is it for them the first time.

The next is a light weight, a fast one—
  A big slashing horse, and a boy ;
Seven five tells he'll not be the last one
  To catch Wakley's eye on the day.
He's an **Arsenal** ; although not a cannon,
  He shoots to the front, straight and true,
Delighting the heart of Will Gannon—
  A shot of the first water, too.

Dunlop does the trick for Dick Donovan,
  And wins him a nice little pile ;
A beautiful mover, and son of an
  Excellent sire. With a smile
Donald Wallace's face shows the pleasure
  He feels when his **Mentor** has won,
And knows that he owns a rare treasure
  In Nightshade's and Swiveller's son.

So ends the long list of Cup races,
  The names of the winners you've seen ;
From Archer to Mentor their paces
  Have varied, some seconds between.
Dunlop bears the palm, for he won it,
  In three twenty-eight and a half ;
Sheet Anchor and Mentor have done it
  In time at which no one can laugh.

Looking back on the flight of the " Master,
  Old Time," as he steadily plies
His scythe, filling fast, and still faster,
  His swathe of life's best families
Of horses and men who have shone in
  The bright, brilliant scenes of the past,
We ponder and see what they've done in
  Their time, from the first to the last.

How the great race has kept on increasing
  In value, as year followed year,
And seems to go on without ceasing,
  Attractive to peasant and peer.
We know we shall miss many faces
  Of owners, and trainers, as well
As artists on pig skin, their places
  Will know them no more, sad to tell !

But while we shall miss and regret them,
  Their mem'ries will cling to us still ;
When the bell rings we must not forget
  them—
  A place in our hearts they will fill.
When we meet on the fifth of November,
  To see the next race for the Cup,
Joe Morrison's form we'll remember,
  But ne'er more see poor Alec's up.

A short space ! A prospect ! ! A tip for
  The Cup of one eight eighty-nine,
In which I may easily trip, for
  The horses whose names brightly shine
In the long list I now see before me,
  Would puzzle an Augur to guess
The first, when the race is all o'er—see
  How I shall attempt, ne'er the less.

In looking at **Carbine**, I know what
  A thoroughbred top weight can do ;
The horse that can beat him will show that
  He is of the first water, too.
When **Wallace** and **White** meet together,
  A race for the dollars is run ;
And Hales and O'Brien show whether
  The horse he rides is the great gun.

To win the big prize takes a flyer,
  He must be a stayer as well—
Be bred from a fleet dam and sire ;
  I know such a horse, and will tell
What his name is, and what his condition,
  I've no need to say any more ;
He'll be trained to a day, his position
  First place, and his name **Singapore**.

John Whiteman.

✠ F. TILLEY, ✠
VICTORIA HOTEL,
BOURKE STREET WEST,
MELBOURNE.

VISITORS TO MELBOURNE!

Do not fail to secure Apartments at

MacGregor's Grand New

HOTEL VICTORIA,

BEACONSFIELD PARADE,

ALBERT PARK, SOUTH MELBOURNE!

NOW OPEN.

'BUSSES—ROYAL ARCADE.   TRAINS—FLINDERS STREET.

Opposite Promenade Pier and Esplanade, and commanding grand view of Bay, and within 15 minutes of General Post Office, Melbourne

Visitors will find all the comforts of a first-class home, sea bathing (hot or cold). A few minutes from Albert Park Railway Station, one minute from Omnibus Stand, which start every five minutes for General Post Office.

This magnificent Hotel, which possesses every modern convenience and comfort, is beautifully furnished, and situated facing the Bay and Esplanade; no expense being spared to make it one of the most complete Hotels in Australasia, and is now open to receive Visitors. Private Suites and Rooms for families, excellent Bedrooms, select Dining, Smoking, and Reading Rooms, splendid Billiard Room, Hot and Cold Baths. Electric Bells in every room throughout the building.

TELEPHONE No. 1523.   TERMS MODERATE.

Application by Telegram or Letter will receive prompt attention.

HOTEL VICTORIA,
BEACONSFIELD PARADE, ALBERT PARK, SOUTH MELBOURNE.

SHEVILL & CO., GENERAL MERCANTILE AUCTIONEERS
House, Land and Estate Agents,

PRELL'S BUILDINGS, Corner of Queen Street and Flinders Lane.

BRANCH OFFICE—32 CHAPEL STREET, SOUTH YARRA.

Sales Held at Rooms. Outdoor Sales Conducted. Valuations Made. Insurance Effected. Advances Made on all Classes of Merchandise and Colonial Produce for Sale or Shipment.

PORT PHILLIP CLUB HOTEL,
FLINDERS STREET, MELBOURNE.

This old established Family Hotel has undergone

← COMPLETE RENOVATION, →

And is now one of the

BEST APPOINTED AND MOST COMFORTABLE HOTELS
IN AUSTRALIA.

T. HUNTER - - Proprietor.

TELEPHONE 387.

The Shamrock Brewing and Malting Co.,

COLLINGWOOD, LIMITED,

VICTORIA STREET, ABBOTSFORD,

Call attention to their Celebrated Bulk

XXX AND XXXX ALES,

And also to their Bottled

EXTRA PALE ALE AND EXTRA BROWN STOUT,

In the manufacture of which none but the Purest and Best Materials are used.—*Vide*
CERTIFICATES from the GOVERNMENT and other WELL-KNOWN ANALYSTS.
NOTE,—Ask for SHAMROCK BRAND.   At all Hotels in Town and Suburbs.
Telephonic Communication with the Brewery.—Telephone 641.

H. C. BOYD, Managing Director.

WILSON, CORBEN & CO.,

25 ELIZABETH STREET - - MELBOURNE.

The Best House in Victoria for

MANTELPIECES, GASFITTINGS, GRATES,

Tiles, Sanitary Ware, &c., &c.

LATEST NOVELTIES BY EVERY STEAMER.

Note the Address—

New Showrooms - - 25 Elizabeth Street, Melbourne
(Near Flinders Street).

Established 1852.

E. A. GOSEWINCKEL,

Successor to KASNER & MOSS,

Practical Optician and Mathematical Instrument Maker,

332 (formerly No. 17) COLLINS STREET W.,

MELBOURNE.

—:o:—

THE SIGHT THOROUGHLY AND SCIENTIFICALLY TESTED.
Oculists' Prescriptions carefully attended to.   Artificial Eyes carefully fitted.
Three First Prize Medals for Workmanship.
Race Glasses in great variety.   Magic Lanterns and Slides on Hire.
Every description of Optical and Mathematical Work repaired by Competent Workmen
on the Shortest Notice.
Spectacles Sent for Repairs Returned by the Following Post.

McLEAN BROTHERS & RIGG,

GENERAL AND FURNISHING IRONMONGERS,

107 to 113 ELIZABETH STREET, MELBOURNE.

Race Glasses, Race Glasses, Race Glasses.   Opera Glasses, Opera Glasses, Opera Glasses.
Picnic Baskets, Luncheon Baskets, Lawn Tennis Rackets, Balls and Nets, Guns, Rifles, English and
American Sporting Requirements and Games of all kinds, Revolvers, Air Guns, Roller Skates.

McLEAN BROTHERS & RIGG, MELBOURNE.

CURRAN'S FAMILY HOTEL,

VICTORIA STREET (top of Swanston St.), MELBOURNE.

EVERY ACCOMMODATION and COMFORT for BOARDERS. Private Sitting
Rooms for Ladies. Charges—6s. per Day ; 25s. per Week. Queensberry-st. Trams,
Omnibusses and Cabs pass the door every minute, *en route* to Wharf and Railway Station.
Mr. CURRAN (late of the Swan Hotel, Stratford) invites Gippsland Visitors.
"The Gippsland Mercury" filed.

A Record of The Melbourne Cup.

INAUGURAL MEETING
1861.
MELBOURNE CUP,

Of 20 sovs., 10 sovs. forfeit, or 5 sovs. if declared, with 200 sovs. added by the Victoria Turf Club. Two miles.

Mr. E. De Mestre's b h ARCHER, 5yrs, 9st 7lbs (Cutts) 1
Mr. J. Henderson's ns br h MORMON, 6yrs, 10st 1lb (Simpson) 2
Mr. Wm. Pearson's bl g PRINCE, aged, 8st (Bishop) 3

Mr. B. Warby's br c Antonelli, 3yrs, 6st 7lbs (Cowan) ; Mr. T. Bavin's gr g Flatcatcher, aged, 9st 3lbs (Perkins) ; Mr. G. Watson's bl g The Moor, aged, 8st 12lbs (Waldock) ; Mr. J. Henderson's ns ch m Despatch, aged, 8st 9lbs (Morrison) ; Mr. De Mestre's b g Inheritor, aged, 8st 7lbs (McCabe) ; Mr. Coldham's br m Twilight, aged, 7st 12lbs (Haynes) ; Mr. J. Coldham's b f Grey Dawn, 4yrs, 7st 12lbs (Yeend) ; Mr. T. Bavin's br c Moscow, 4yrs, 7st 12lbs ; Mr. W. C. Yuille's gr g Toryboy, 4yrs, 7st 11lbs (Cooke) ; Mr. J. Hume's bl m Black Bess, 6yrs, 7st 11lbs (Monaghan) ; Mr. J. Henderson ns f Medora, 3yrs, 7st (J. Henderson) ; Mr. J. Henderson ns ch g Sorcerer, 3yrs, 6st 9lbs (Hughes) ; Mr. W. C. Yuille's br c Eagle's Plume, 3yrs, 6st 7lbs (Lankey) ; Mr. Cole's ro g Fireaway, 3yrs, 6st 6lbs (Howard) ; Mr. E. Coleman's br f Lucy Ashton, 3yrs, 6st 4lbs (Davis).

Eagle's Plume weighed out and mounted, but after taking his preliminary canter was returned to the saddling paddock and sent straight home.

Archer,

a magnificent bright bay, standing 16·3, by William Tell—Maid of the Oaks, came with a great reputation from Sydney, but notwithstanding his size and condition, he failed to inspire general confidence, as it was thought the Victorian champion, Mormon, was more than a match for the visitor.

The rival merits of the formidable pair were eagerly discussed, but the confidence of the Victorians increasing as the hour of starting arrived, the Sydney party ceased to support their horse, and Mormon, Despatch and Toryboy appeared to be the general favorites.

Betting 7 to 2 agst. Mormon, 4 to 1 agst. Despatch, 9 to 1 agst. Toryboy, 5 to 1 agst. Archer, 8 to 1 agst. Inheritor, 8 to 1 agst. Flatcatcher, 12 to 1 agst. others.

Before starting Twilight bolted, and went all round the course in fine style before she could be pulled up.

After one false start the horses got well away together, Flatcatcher taking the lead, Archer next, and then came Mormon, Medora, Prince and Despatch, the others in a ruck. As they rounded the turn into the straight Flatcatcher was two lengths ahead of Archer, and the latter a length ahead of the field. At this point a lamentable accident occurred through Twilight, Medora and Despatch falling, and of the three only Twilight arose, her rider sticking bravely to the reins. She, however, eventually got loose and careered away from the course.

While the spectators hastily removed the injured jockeys and horses, the remaining fourteen runners dashed past the stand at a tremendous rate, the front rank being composed of Mormon, Archer, Fireaway and Antonelli.

At the river side the two Sydney horses, Archer and Inheritor, were in front, but the latter soon beat a retreat, and the light weighted Antonelli became the immediate follower of the great Sydney crack, who, still forcing the pace past the abattoirs, left a spread-eagle field behind him contending for place honours. As the New South Wales hero came on well away from his horses, Mormon drew gradually forward, and Toryboy fell back beaten. On entering the straight running Antonelli hung out signals of distress, and Prince supplanted him. The race was virtually over a quarter of a mile from home, the Sydney horse coming in at last an easy winner by several lengths, Mormon second, Prince third, and Antonelli close up.

Time—3 min. 52 secs.

THE ACCIDENT.

It appears to be extremely difficult to arrive at a correct solution of the cause of the melancholy accident ; the riders themselves being unable to give any reliable account of the affair. It was said Despatch got her fore legs entangled with the hind legs of some other horse and fell, Medora and Twilight falling over her. Other accounts state that Medora was the first to fall, either by slip or cannon with Despatch ; then the latter fell headlong over her, and Twilight followed, all three, with their riders, coming heavily to the ground.

Upon examination, it was found Despatch had apparently broken her back, and her rider, Joe Morrison, received a compound comminuted fracture of the left arm, the bone coming through the skin in two places.

All agree that the unfortunate occurrence was only an accident, and that no person was blameable for the deplorable result, which threw a cloud over the remainder of the day's proceedings.

After this lamentable occurrence it was decided to alter the position of the starting point of the race by extending the straight running to about a distance inside the training ground, and thus, by avoiding the turn, obviate the probability of another such accident.

On 13th November,

1862,

Mr. Watson marshalled the horses for the first time at the now well-known starting place. Of the 21 horses that he then got into line,

Archer,

in blooming condition, was installed first favourite, for the New South Welshmen had Mormon's measure, and this time would not be denied. Tallyrand, too, had supporters, and he and Archer, bracketted together, were backed against the field at even money. Mormon was fresh and full of life, his beautiful action being again and again the subject of loudly expressed admiration. Ebor and Musidora had admirers, especially the latter; and Camden had numerous friends, but a "doubtful" leg kept down the enthusiasm of The Colonel's stable.

As though showing their appreciation of the improvements to the course the whole twenty dashed off to a beautiful start at the first attempt, and the magnificent sight, now so familiar, but then viewed for the first time, drew forth repeated and earnest expressions of gratification from the spectators.

The Colonel and Dun Dolo were slightly in advance as they raced up the straight, with Cedric, Camden, and Mormon just heading the ruck, while Archer and Lady Constance brought up the rear, only under different circumstances.

At the river side the field began to spread, and presently there was nearly a distance between the leading horses and Archer, who was still kept in the back ground. The Colonel continued to make the running at a severe pace, with Dun Dolo on his quarter, while Archer, leaving poor Lady Constance hope-lessly last, rapidly passed the cluster of horses behind the leading ruck. Before reaching the abattoirs The Colonel's leg gave way, and Dun Dolo also retired, leaving Mormon and Camden in possession, the latter slightly leading. Archer closed upon Mormon, and then passed Camden, who, after making an effort to live with the favorite, dropped back beaten. The race was over half a mile from home, Archer coming away from his toiling followers and again winning with the greatest ease by six or eight lengths, while brave old Mormon, beating Camden from the distance, for the second time followed the Sydney horse home.

The value of the stakes this year was 830 sovs., being a sweepstakes of 20 sovs. each, 10 forfeit, or 5 sovs. if declared, with 200 sovs. added.

The runners were—

Mr. De Mestre's b h ARCHER, 6yrs, 10st 2lbs (Cutts) 1

Mr. Keighran ns b h MORMON, aged, 9st 12lbs (Simpson) 2

Mr. J. Henderson ns b c CAMDEN, 4yrs, 8st 7lbs (Morrison) 3

Mr. J. Tait's ch g Tallyrand, 6yrs, 9st 12lbs, including 5lbs extra (Ashworth); Mr. Bavin's gr g Flatcatcher, aged, 9st 4lbs (Carter); Mr. Jeffrey's ch h The Colonel, 5yrs, 9st (Waldock); Mr. Bavin's b h Moscow, 5yrs, 8st 4lbs (Monaghan); Mr. Lang's br h Dauntless, 5yrs, 8st 2lbs (Henderson); Mr. Wilson's b c Ebor, 4yrs, 8st 2lbs (Bates); Mr. Hughes' b m Susan, 5yrs, 8st (Robinson); Mr. McCormick's gr g Toryboy, 5yrs, 7st 13lbs (Trainor); Mr. Lamb's b c Paul Pry, 4yrs, 7st 13lbs (Cousins); Mr. Benyon's b c Bray, aged, 7st 12lbs (Solloway); Mr. Lamb's b g Attila, aged, 7st 12lbs (Gill); Mr. Harper's br f Lady Constance, 4yrs, 7st 11lbs (W. Perkins); Mr. Lamb's ch g Cedric, 5yrs, 7st 7lbs (Davies); Messrs. Wood and Kirk's bl g Dun Dolo, 4yrs, 7st (Waterman); Mr. Wilson's br f Musidora, 3yrs, 6st 3lbs (Grimwood); Mr. Baillie's br g O.K., 3yrs, 5st 7lbs, carried 6st 2lbs (Redman); Mr. Henry's bl c Ithuriel, 3yrs, 5st 4lbs, carried 5st 8lb (Howard).

2 to 1 agst. Archer, 4 to 1 each agst. Mormon, Tallyrand and Camden, 10 to 1 agst. Musidora, 16 to 1 each agst. Ebor, The Colonel, Paul Pry, 25 to 1 each agst. Bray, Attila and Dun Dolo, 50 to 1 the others.

That Archer was the best horse of his time seems to have been generally conceded. In fact, many who remember him assert that he was the finest horse Australia ever produced, and though it is difficult to institute comparisons, still it must be remembered that while carrying 9st 7lbs in the first race and 10st 2lbs in the second he literally romped home, the easiest of winners on each occasion. The time was certainly slow, but circumstances were not so favourable for racing then as they are now. Besides, it was never known what Archer really could do. That

THOMAS GAUNT,
WATCHMAKER, JEWELLER
And Optician,

337 BOURKE STREET,

Corner Royal Arcade.

CHRONOGRAPHS and FIELD GLASSES of
Unsurpassed Quality.

DUN'S
MANGER
SALT,
FOR HORSES.

**This SALT possesses a Peculiar Virtue in giving TONE
to the SYSTEM and RELISH for FOOD.**

It induces a healthy flow of saliva, so necessary to the assistance of
digestion, the proper exercise of which function is sure to promote

HEALTH, VIGOR, GOOD TEMPER & SPIRIT.

Its Tonic Properties are well known in English stables,
where it is extensively used.

T. W. NORRIS, Proprietor,
242 LITTLE COLLINS STREET
(Opposite City Watch House),
MELBOURNE.

Trained by owner   ARCHER, 1861-2.   Ridden by J. Cutts
Mr. E. De Mestre

Trained by owner   BANKER, 1863.   Ridden by Chifney
Mr. J. Harper

we had nothing to race with him is certain, as he was never called upon to fairly extend himself in either of the Cups he won. Trainor, who rode Toryboy in the second Cup race, mentions that soon after passing the abattoirs Billy Simpson expressed his belief that Mormon would win, and as he forged past the little grey, "It's my day out, Trainor," the crack jockey of his time exclaimed; but scarcely were the words uttered when they beheld the mighty Archer sweeping past on the extreme outside at a pace that soon left them all toiling in the rear. Cutts knew he could better afford to run right round his horses than risk the chance of being blocked.

This wonderful performer seems to have struck terror into the hearts of owners, for in the succeeding year only twenty-five entries were received for the race, and the handicappers sought to neutralize the effects of Archer's monopoly by imposing the crushing weight of 11st 4lbs. Even then Mr. De Mestre thought there was a probability of his being able to appropriate Cup number three. But the fates befriended Victorian owners, for Archer's acceptance arrived too late, and neither he nor any other representative from New South Wales put in an appearance. As a consequence, the race lost much of its interest, for only a miserable field of seven competitors came to the post in

1863,

and the stakes dwindled down to 510 sovs. Mr. Hurtle Fisher's English filly, Rose of Denmark, was installed first favorite, not without reason, considering she was weighted at only 5st 9lbs, and her party were very sanguine.

Barwon, in one of his usual fits of playfulness, managed to kick Sam Waldock on the thigh very severely, but he rode him notwithstanding.

Musidora scarcely looked in such good form as on previous occasions, but Mr. Lang's filly, Aruma, was in excellent trim, and after the preliminary canter she was specially fancied.

Falcon looked decidedly sick and sorry, and it was evidently not his day out.

The three year old bay colt,

Banker,

by Boiardo—Jeannette, and own brother to Barwon, was, strange to say, almost lost sight of, except by the knowing few.

The race was a sweepstakes of 20 sovs. each, 10 sovs. forfeit, or 5 sovs. if declared, with 200 sovs. added by the Victoria Turf Club.

Mr. J. Harper's b c BANKER, 3yrs. 5st 9lb (Chifney) 1
Mr. Jas. Wilson's br f MUSIDORA, 4yrs, 8st 5lb (Fountain) 2
Mr. Hurtle Fisher's ch f ROSE OF DENMARK 3yrs, 5st 9lb (Tothill) 3

Mr. J. Harper's b c Barwon. 4yrs, 9st 5lbs, 5lbs extra (Waldock) ; Mr. Dowling's ch g Falcon. 6yrs, 8st 13lbs, 5lbs extra (Morrison) ; Mr. J. Morrison's b g Shillelagh, aged, 7st 7lb (Howard) ; Mr Lang's b f Aruma 3yrs, 6st 6lb (T. Pullar).

Betting 2 to 1 agst Rose of Denmark, 2 to 1 agst Musidora, 5 to 1 agst Barwon and Aruma, 8 to 1 agst Falcon and Shillelagh, 10 to 1 agst Banker.

The seven starters, through being wide apart, appeared to get away on anything but even terms, though they actually left all together, and galloped so for a couple of hundred yards, then Banker rushed to the front with his featherweight, Aruma, Rose of Denmark, Musidora and Barwon (hard held) keeping him company in the order named. A sheet could have covered them as they dashed past the stand at a rattling pace, Aruma, who had taken up the running, having a little the best of it until rounding the turn, where she lost a good deal of ground, and gave the Rose of Denmark a temporary advantage.

The latter, favoured by her light weight, led along the river side at a tremendous pace, Banker, Barwon and Aruma being her nearest attendants.

At the abattoirs, Banker went up to the Rose, and Aruma and Barwon following suit, an interesting struggle for the leadership took place. Banker ultimately succeeded in getting to the front as they neared the turn, the other three being in close attendance.

Musidora then made a move forward, and soon disposing of Aruma and Barwon, took third place as Banker entered the straight two lengths clear of Mr. Fisher's mare.

A busy race ensued from the distance, which resulted in Banker winning by a good length, Musidora second, Rose of Denmark two lengths away third.

Time—3min. 44secs.

Rose of Denmark did not go to scale, so Barwon was weighed in as third.

The Melbourne Cup now passed through a critical period. There were two clubs—the Jockey Club and the Turf Club—among the members of which dissension was rife. However they eventually agreed to amalgamate, and all lovers of sport rejoiced when in

1864

the Melbourne Cup entered upon a new era. On Thursday, 3rd November, of that year, the first regular meeting was held under the management of the newly-formed Victorian Racing Club.

Heavy showers of rain fell during the day, but notwithstanding the inclemency of the weather there was an especially good attendance.

The difficulties of the deep places near the training ground brought many a joke, or something worse, from the drivers of cars or the occupants of seats in those overloaded conveyances.

The want of railway conveniences was sadly felt, and the journey, as undertaken by the general public, was a thing not to be enjoyed. It required the spirits of a "Mark Tapley" to enable a man to be jolly in an overcrowded conveyance, with a walk before him through the muddiest and worst parts of the way to the course.

The stake on this occasion amounted to about 800 sovs., and was won by Mr. Hurtle Fisher's

Lantern,

by Muscovado—dam Nightlight.

The winner was fairly backed, being looked upon as a promising colt, but few supposed that the 3 year old would show his celebrated competitors his heels in the style he did.   His preliminary canter revealed the fact that he possessed a remarkably long and quick stride, which won him many friends.

Roebuck was installed first favorite, but his appearance did not quite satisfy his backers.

Fleur-de-lis, however, was in splendid condition, and a glance at her was sufficient to raise the expectations of her supporters.

Rose of Denmark was well supported, and her performance justified the confidence of her friends; while the appearance of the Flying Buck gave rise to the hope that he would that day merit the high opinion formed of him after his wonderful victory in 1859.

Mr. Hurtle Fisher's br c LANTERN, 3yrs, 6st 3lbs (Davis) 1
Mr. Pears' b c POET, 4yrs, 8st 7lbs (Perkins) 2
Mr. H. Fisher's ch f ROSE OF DEN-MARK, 4yrs, 8st 3lbs (Howard) ... 3

Mr. Harper's b h Barwon, 5yrs, 9st 9lbs (Morrison) ; Mr. P. Dowling's Falcon, aged, 9st 9lbs (Henderson) ; Mr. J. Wilson's br m Musidora, 5yrs, 9st 4lbs (Simpson) ; Mr. James' b h Ebor, 6yrs, 8st 12lbs (Fountain) ; Mr. Keighran's b g Playboy, aged, 8st 9lbs, (Dowling) ; Mr. Cook's b c Glenyuille 4yrs, 8st 7lbs (Holmes) ; Mr. Harper's b c Banker, 4yrs, 8st 7lbs (S. Waldock) ; Mr. T. Henty's br h Saturn, 6yrs, 8st 2lbs (Lang) ; Mr. Davies's b g Flying Buck, aged, 7st 9lbs (Carter) ; Mr. H. Fisher's ch f Chrysolite, 4yrs, 7st 8lbs (Redmond) ; Mr. C. Day's br g Attila, aged, 7st 3lbs (Parslow) ; Mr. Holmes' br m Fleur-de-lis, 5yrs, 7st (Grimwood) ; Mr. P. Dowling's br c Roebuck, 3yrs, 6st 10lbs (Bateman) ; Mr. W. Robinson's br c Freestone, 6st 10lbs (Green) ; Mr. W. Treacy's ch f Gwendoline, 3yrs, 5st 12lbs (Pullar) ; Mr. Jeffrey's ch g Bedouin ; 3ys, 5st 9lbs (Chifney).

Betting : 7 to 2 agst. Roebuck, 4 to 1 agst. Musidora, 6 to 1 agst. Barwon, 8 to 1 each agst. Falcon, Saturn, and Fleur-de-lis ; 10 to 1 each agst. Banker, Flying Buck, Freestone, Lantern, Rose of Denmark ; 15 to 1 Glenyuille and Ebor. 20 to 1 any other.

After a delay of some minutes, caused by a heavy shower passing over the course, a fair start was effected at the first attempt, and the large field went away upon nearly equal terms.   Saturn, Freestone, Lantern, Barwon and Poet were the first to show in advance, and they led the field past the stand at a good pace, Roebuck and Flying Buck bringing up the rear.

Saturn led round the turn with the others close up, all going well, with the exception of Flying Buck, who suddenly dropped out altogether.   All the horses ran in a complete cluster for the next half mile at a rattling pace, Saturn maintaining his lead to the abattoirs, where he compounded and gave way to his immediate followers, Poet and Lantern, who led alternately, while some of the ruck moved forward, Gwendoline, Musidora, Banker and Rose of Denmark particularly improving their positions.

Lantern, Poet and Rose of Denmark entered the straight some distance in advance of the field.   A very pretty finish ensued, Lantern eventually passing the post under the judges chair, a length and a half in front of Poet, who finished next to the rails ; Rose of Denmark a good third, with Gwendoline, Ebor and Musidora so close together

LANTERN, 1864.
Mr. Hurtle Fisher

Trained by W. Filgate   Ridden by S. Davis

TORYBOY, 1865.
Mr. B.C. Marshall.

Trained by P. Miley   Ridden by Kavanagh

that it was impossible to state which was actually fourth.

Time—3min. 48secs.

Mr. Hurtle Fisher had previously won the Ascot Vale stakes, and when the luck of the Maribyrnong stables was repeated with Lantern in the Cup, it produced an enthusiastic demonstration at the success of this worthy sportsman.

The following year another staunch supporter of the turf was unfortunate in failing to score a win with that grand horse, Panic, who in

1865

ran second to the lively little grey gelding,

Toryboy,

aged, by Wollaton—dam, Fair Ellen; and game as this little horse proved himself to be, it is impossible not to sympathise with those who doubted if the principal race of the meeting should be based upon conditions that placed a horse imported at the price of 1500 guineas on a level with a nice neat, game little pony.

However, the services of Panic were largely availed of in after years, for the race gave him an opportunity of showing what he could do, and he has become famous, while the winner's name has long since sunk to the oblivion of a mere record.

Toryboy started with odds of 20 to 1 against him, Rose of Denmark being the favourite at 5 to 1 against, and 6 and 7 to 1 were laid against Panic, Poet and Angler; 12 to 1 each against Playboy, Victoria, Mozart; 16 to 1 Riverina and Alexandra; 20 to 50 to 1 the others.

Mr. Keighran gave the twenty-three an excellent start, and when they had traversed a furlong or so Panic could be distinguished in advance in the centre of the cluster, Frolic, Minstrel, Playboy, Oriflamme, Poet and The Miller all lying close up.

Frolic secured a slight advantage of Panic and Poet at the stand, but then Minstrel rushed to the front, though he as quickly retired again in favour of the Tasmanian champion, who forced the running at a slashing pace, still closely attended by the harmonic trio, Poet, Minstrel and Songster. The first named of the three broke down, however, near the abattoirs, and the other two almost immediately cried content. Toryboy then worked his way towards the front, wearing all his field down except Panic and Frolic, who contested the lead with him till half a mile from home, where Frolic fell back, and the race was left to the heaviest and lightest weighted of the aged horses.

The champion made a gallant effort, answering in the gamest manner every call of Morrison, but the 1ost told its tale, and the son of Alarm was eventually beaten by the determined featherweight by two lengths, Riverina third a similar distance behind Panic; then came Angler, Cadland and Musidora.

Time—3 min. 44 secs.

A piece of plate, value 100 sovs., accompanied the usual sweepstakes of 20 sovs., 10 sovs. forfeit, 5 sovs. if declared, with 200 sovs. added. Value of stake, about 950 sovs.

Mr. B. C. Marshall's gr g TORYBOY, aged, Wollaton – Fair Ellen, 7st (Kavenagh) 1
Mr. P. Dowling's br h PANIC, aged, Alarm– Queen of Beauty, 10st (Morrison) 2
Mr. W. Hutton's b m RIVERINA, 5yrs, Reubens— , 7st 7lbs (Yeomans) 3

Mr. I. Pear's c h Poet, 5yrs, 9st 6lbs (Ashworth) ; Mr. D. Kennedy's ch h Oriflamme, 5yrs, 9st (Lang); Mr. J. Wilson's br m Musidora, 6yrs, 9st (Fountain); Mr. P. J. Keighran's b g Playboy, aged, 8st 11lbs (Carter); Mr. W. A. Wetton's b g Minstrel, 5yrs, 8st 7lbs (Waldock); Mr. I. Pear's ch g Songster, 4yrs, 8st 7lbs (Stanley) ; Mr. W. Pearson's b g Viscount, aged, 8st 5lbs (R. Clark) ; Mr. W. Field's b m Ellen, aged, 8st 5lbs (Winter) ; Mr. Hurtle Fisher's ch m Rose of Denmark, 5yrs, 8st 3lbs (Goodman); Mr. F. Hobson's b g Jule-cum-Sneezer, aged, 8st (Bishop) ; Mr. W. C. Yuille's b f Victoria, 4yrs, 8st (Cooke); Mr. J. Field's b c Mahratta, 4yrs, 7st 13lbs (P. Gill) ; Mr. W. Field's br g Cadland, 4yrs, 7st 10lbs (Chifney) ; Mr. J. Armstrong's bl g Mozart, aged, 7st. 9lbs (Hill) ; Mr. Warren's br m Shadow, aged, 7st. 7lb (T. Handley) ; Mr. P. Dowling's b c Frolic, 3yrs, 6st 12lb (Mitchell) ; Mr. H. Fisher's br c Angler, 3yrs, 6st 5lb (Davis) ; Mr. H. G. Bowler's b f Nightshade, 3yrs, 6st (Haysted) ; Mr. W. J. Fariss' gr f Alexandra, 3yrs, 5st 12lbs (Davis).

The despised Toryboy, although not much more than a pony, was a thorough racehorse. Knowing ones laughed and would not listen when it was rumored that a week or more before the race he had covered the distance at Flemington in 3m. 44secs. However, they opened their eyes when they saw him come through his horses and defeat the great Panic, who by the bye ran away with Morrison at the beginning of the race, and then carried him home such a glorious second.

The Melbourne Cup was now steadily growing in public favor, in fact the great event had come to be proverbially known as the people's race. But never had it so fully established its claim to the flattering title as in

1866,

when it attracted no less than twenty-eight competitors, all generally superior to any previous fields, and amongst them came one, The Barb, prepared to dispute for the pride of place with the best of his predecessors.

The spirit of rivalry was abroad. There was throughout all the betting fever this year a strong disposition to back New South Wales against Victoria and the other colonies who were represented.

From first to last the Sydney party were confident in the superiority of their cattle, and as a reward for their confidence and pluck,

The Barb,

by Sir Hercules—Young Gulnare, carrying more than his weight for age vanquished the best horses the colonies could muster.

The Barb had been considered all but dead, and the money was piled on his stable companion, Falcon; but he came to life again in a marvellous manner, and won in the fastest time recorded up to that date.

The start was delayed owing to Seagull and Shenandoah bolting, the latter unseating her rider.

On this occasion the start was effected with two flags—Mr. Keighran in the rear with one piece of bunting signalling the start to Mr. Pearson in front, and the latter repeating it to the riders, when the field, with the exception of Cowra, dashed away well together.

When, however, Mr. Bagot's filly did commence to move, it was with the evident determination to make up for lost time, and, as Tim Whiffler led the field past the stand, she followed them at a pace that clearly indicated she meant to be in it. But, though managing to get on terms with the company as they flew round the turn, the effort had been too severe, and she shot her

bolt just as the Barb drew up and assumed the lead from Glenyuille, who had supplanted Tim Whiffler, the latter being third, Barwon fourth, with the others well up. In this order the mingled mass of flying colors rushed along the back of the course, but at the abattoirs, Exile drew on the leaders, and he and The Barb, raced stride for stride, with Sydney Falcon third, and Playboy fourth. At the home turn the "black demon" held a slight advantage of Exile, and it became evident the race lay between these two. A magnificent struggle home ensued, and, as they passed the far end of the stand, the issue was still in doubt, but the Sydney colt running under the whip from the distance, gamely answered every call, and was ultimately landed a winner by a short neck, Sydney Falcon next, and Seagull, Playboy and Tim Whiffler well up. Time, 3min. 43secs.

The Judge, Mr. J. G. Dougharty, did not place a third horse. However, the stewards took upon themselves to rectify the mistake, and placed Sydney Falcon third, a proceeding to which many objected, being afterwards supported in their opinion by Admiral Rouse.

A piece of plate, valued 100 sovs., again accompanied the usual sweepstakes and 200 sovs. added money, the whole stake amounting to 1080 sovs.

Mr. J. Tait's b c THE BARB, 3yrs, 6st 9lbs (Davis) 1
Mr. P. J. Keighran's b g EXILE, aged, 7st 10lbs (Cavenagh) 2
Mr. J. Tait's ch g FALCON, 5yrs, 8st 2lbs (Stanley) not placed 3
Mr. C. B. Fisher's b m Lady Heron, 4yrs, 8st 7lbs (Morrison); Mr. W. Craig's Tim Whiffler, 4yrs, 8st 8lbs (Chifney); Mr. E. M. Bagot's gr f Cowra. 4yrs, 8st 7lbs (Stevens); Mr. J. Cleeland's b h Barwon, aged, 8st 7lbs (S. Haynes); Mr. G. Wright's ch g Songster, 5yrs, 8st 6lbs (Parslow); Mr. T. T. Lewis' ch g Falcon, aged, 8st 6lb. (Bateman); Mr. W. Pearson's br g Sparrowhawk, 5yrs, 8st 5lbs (Harvey); Mr. J. Tait's ch g Warwick, 5yrs, 8st 5lbs (Holmes); Mr. S. Thompson's b g Woodman, aged, 8st 4lbs (Bishop); Mr. J. Wilson's b m Musidora, aged, 8st 4lbs (McDonald); Mr. W. Craig's br m Miss Fisher, 4yrs, 8st (Carter); Mr. P. J. Keighran's b g Playboy, aged, 8st (Waterman); Mr. W. Pearson's b g Viscount, aged, 7st 12lbs (Mason); Mr. W. C. Yuille's gr g Toryboy, aged, 7st 8lbs (Green); Mr. G. Watson's b g Minstrel, 6yrs, 7st 5lbs (Gregory); Mr. A. McDonald's bl g Dun Dolo, 6yrs, 7st 5lbs (Tyrrell); Mr. J. Cleeland's gr m Shenandoah, 6yrs, 7st

G. F. PICKLES & SONS,

Have now on view that Magnificent Display of Fine-Art

Carriages, Buggies, Private Waggonettes, &c.,

Exhibited by them at the recent Show of the National Agricultural Society of Victoria. A collection unanimously pronounced as the best ever seen in Australia. We were awarded

16 PRIZES, including amongst them the **GRAND PRIZE,**

Only Gold Medal—for the Best Carriage, a record unequalled by any other firm.

These awards, coupled with our recent victories against the world at Centennial Exhibition, not only show the vast resources at our command, but an organisation of skill and science unattainable by any other firm in this country.

INSPECTION INVITED.

G. F. PICKLES & SONS,

CARRIAGE BUILDERS,

By Special Appointment to His Excellency the Governor.

REPOSITORY—

340 to 346 LATROBE STREET, WEST,

MANUFACTORY—

32, 34, 36 BRUNSWICK STREET, FITZROY.

Fred Woodhouse, sen. Pinxt.   R. J. Woodhouse Lith.

Trained by owner   **THE BARB, 1866.**   Ridden by W. Davis
Mr John Tait

Fred Woodhouse, senr. Pinxt.   R. J. Woodhouse Lith.

Trained by owner   **TIM WHIFFLER, 1867.**   Ridden by Driscoll.
Mr De Mestre.

2lbs (Puller); Mr. J. Armstrong's Mozart, aged, 7st 1lb (A. Hill); Mr. H. D. Parr's br f Deception, 5yrs, 7st (Parr); Mr. L. L. Smith's b g Glenyuille 6yrs, (Hill); Mr. T. Henty's br g Coventry, 4yrs, 6st 12lbs (Griffin); Mr. C. B. Fisher's br f Seagull, 3yrs, 6st 7lb (Hill); Mr. L L. Smith's gr g Perfection, 5yrs, 6st 4lb (Davies); Mr. S. Waldock's b c Lunatic, 3yrs, 5st 8lbs (Howell); Mr. W. J. Fariss' b c Solitaire, 3yrs, 5st 8lbs (Bennett).

Betting: 6 to 1 agst The Barb, 7 to 1 agst Falcon (Sydney), 8 to 1 each Tim Whiffler, Lady Heron, and Seagull, 12 to 1 each Toryboy and Deception. 20 to 50 to 1 others.

Mr. John Tait was overwhelmed with congratulations, and every Australian who knew anything about a horse became enthusiastic over the "black demon." When he won the Champion race on New Year's Day, 1867, in 5m. 38sec. for 3 miles, thus putting all previous records in the shade, it was proposed to send him to England, and many sportsmen must regret that the project was not carried out, for that he was a veritable clinker is beyond dispute.

It had now become a settled idea that the "Cup" should be the event in which the best horses of each colony should try their mettle.

New South Wales had established a supremacy which her sportsmen were determined to maintain; for, as if Mr. John Tait could not give trouble enough, Mr. De Mestre must needs drop on us once more. It seemed to be only a question as to which of these gentlemen was to carry off the prize of

1867.

However, it did not quite resolve itself into a match between their representatives, as Fireworks failed to carry the yellow and black into a place, while Mr. De Mestre's

Tim Whiffler,

by New Warrior—Cinderella, romped home an easy winner by two lengths in four seconds less time than it occupied The Barb to do the journey.

5 to 2 was laid against the winner at starting; 3 to 1 against Fireworks; whilst 10, 12 and 20 to 1 were laid against Privateer, Glencoe and Exile respectively; 30 to 1 against Queen of Hearts, who gamely answering every call, beat Exile for second place by a length.

Exile's performances were brought to a tragic close a few months later when he fell dead after winning the Ballarat Cup.

Sydney Falcon was well supported by many who imagined that he was the peg John Tait intended to hang his hat on; for all that, Fireworks made his toilet under the immediate supervision of his owner.

Tim Whiffler's coat shone like satin; his quarters appeared one mass of muscle as he walked about, seemingly confident, that if blood and condition went for anything his victory was assured.

Mr. E. De Mestre's b h TIM WHIFFLER, by New Warrior ——, 5yrs, 8st 11lbs, 3lbs extra (Driscoll)... 1

Mr. S. Waldock's br f QUEEN OF HEARTS, 3yrs, 5st 10lbs, carried 5st 12lbs (Bennet) 2

Mr. D. Melhado's b g EXILE, aged, 7st 10lbs (Waterman) 3

Mr. J. Tait's ch c, 3yrs, 6st 4lbs (Crocker); Mr. W. Craig's b h Tim Whiffler, 5yrs, 8st 8lbs (Morrison); Mr. J. Tait's ch g Falcon, 6yrs, 8st 7lbs (Stanley); Mr. W. Field's b g Strop, aged, 8st 7lbs (Gill); Mr. E. M. Bagot's gr m Cowra, 5yrs, 8st 7lbs (Thompson); Mr. C. B Fisher's br h Smuggler, 5yrs, 9st 3lbs (A. Davis); Mr. W. Craig's b g Nimblefoot, 4yrs, 8st 1lb (Carter); Mr. J. Cleeland's b h Barwon, aged, 7st 12lbs. carried 8st 1lb (Cooke); Mr. Adcock's b h Crusader, 4yrs, 7st 10lbs (Nunn); Mr. R. Pring's b h North Australian, 4yrs, 7st 9lbs (Holmes); Mr. W. Pearson's b g Sparrowhawk, 6yrs, 7st 7lbs (Griffin); Mr. J. Holmes' b g Woodman, aged, 7st 7lbs (Pullar); Mr. J. Lamb's ch g Cedric, aged, 7st 6lbs (Tunstall); Mr. F. Hobson's b m Poetess, 5yrs, 7st 6lbs (A. Hill); Mr. J. Whitehead's b m Mary Ann, aged, 7st 2lbs (J. Hill); Mr. J. Walker's gr g Toryboy, aged, 7st (S. Davis); Mr. Cleeland's gr m Shenandoah, aged, 6st 10lbs, carried 6st 13lbs (Alf. Hill); Mr. J. Rule's br g Privateer, aged, 6st 8lbs (H. Taylor); Mr. J. Tait's b c Fireworks, 3yrs, 6st 7lbs (Greene); Mr. F. Howell's b m Lady Jane. 4yrs, 6st 5lbs (J. Taylor); Mr. J. Holme's gr g Protection, 6yrs, 6st, carried 6st 5lbs (Francis); Mr. L. L. Smith's b f Lancashire Witch, 3yrs, 5st 13lbs, carried 6st 2lbs (Adderley); Mr. G. Lewis's b c Rip Van Winkle, 3yrs, 5st 2lbs (Mathieson); Mr. C. B. Fisher's b or br f The Fly, 3yrs, 5st 9lbs (Jamieson).

Mr. Watson wielded the starter's flag on this occasion, and was fortunate in getting his horses away on equal terms, with the exception of the ever troublesome Shenandoah and Lancashire Witch. Melbourne Tim was the first to show in front, attended by Toryboy, Exile, Barwon, Sydney Tim, Queen of Hearts, and Rip Van Winkle in close order.

Passing the stand, Rip had a slight lead of Barwon, then came Toryboy and Sparrowhawk, with the others all close together, the last two being Fly and Fireworks. Along the river, Toryboy went to the front, closely followed by Exile, but at the back of the course the latter assumed the lead, the rest coming on in a cluster till entering the straight, when

Sydney Tim got alongside Exile; Queen of Hearts, Toryboy, Sparrowhawk, Strop and Cowra being close at their heels. Glencoe then made his effort, and running on the outside, got into fourth position.

At the distance, Sydney Tim shot out, and Queen of Hearts, challenging Exile, took second place, while Mr. De Mestre's horse, going very comfortably, won by two lengths, Exile third, Glencoe fourth, Melbourne Tim fifth. ·

Time—3min. 39secs.

The increasing popularity of the meeting was now being shown weeks and even months before the event came off by the way the pieces were put down in

1868.

The first to come into favor were North Australian and Bylong. Mr. Hurtle Fisher's pair, Ragpicker and Little Fish were looked upon as likely to uphold the credit of Victoria, although not a few pinned their faith to the flighty but speedy Shenandoah, while other cracks such as The Barb and the Victorian Tim Whiffler and North Australian, being struck out for various causes, Sydney Tim, the victor of '67, went up in the betting. The idea had gone abroad that Mr. De Mestre had a *penchant* for appropriating two cups in succession, and that the redoubted Archer's performances were to be repeated by Tim Whiffler.

In the meantime, Mr. John Tait, though not this time startling the community with a second Barb, was yet doing quiet, steady work with a handsome chestnut son of Lord of the Hills—Queen of Clubs,

Glencoe,

and his performances in his own country had sufficiently impressed the handicappers for them to impose on him the respectable steadier of 8st 12lbs.

The value of the stakes this year had increased to 1260 sovs., being a sweep of 20 sovs., with 300 sovs. added. The starters were—

Mr. J. Tait's ch h GLENCOE, 4 yrs, by Lord of the Hills, 9st 11b, including 3lb penalty (Stanley) 1
Mr. W. Field's b g STROP, aged, 7st 10lo (Walsh) 2
Mr. J. Cleeland's gr m SHENANDOAH, aged, 7st 5lo (Pullar) 3

The following also ran :—Mr. E. De Mestre's b h Tim Whiffler, 6 yrs, 10st 4lb (J. Kean) ; Mr. P. J. Keighran's br m Seagull, 5yrs 8st (Waterman); Mr. J. Keighran's b g Shrimpy, aged, 8st (Donnelly) ; Mr. W. Gray's b g Nimblefoot, 5yrs, 7st 12lb (J. Carter) ; Mr. W. Lee's ch m Gulnare, 6yrs, 7st 10lbs, including 3lb penalty (G. Thompson) ; Mr. W. Lee's ch h Bylong, 5yrs, 7st 7lbs (Bennett) ; Mr. L. L. Smith's b m Lady Manners Sutton, 5yrs, 7st 6lbs (Adderly) ; Mr. H. Fisher's br h Little Fish, 4yrs, 7st 6lbs (Davis); Mr. J. Cleeland's b h Barwon, aged, 7st 5lb (Sullivan); Mr. P. J. Keighran's b f Sylvia, 4yrs, 7st 5lb, carried 7st 7lbs (Atkin) ; Mr. J. Haimes' b g Tasman, aged, 7st 2lbs (Mathieson) ; Mr. H. W. Jellett's br g Snip, aged, 7st (Taylor) ; Mr. T. Ryan's b g Cupbearer, aged, 6st 13lbs, carried 8st 3lbs (Tothill) ; Mr. J. Whitehead's b m Mary Ann, aged, 6st 11lbs, carried 7st 4lbs (Goodie) ; Mr. J. Haimes' b h Smolensko, aged, 6st 10lb, carried 6st 13lbs (Mitchell) ; Mr J. Lamb's bh Booyoolee, 6yrs, 6st 10lbs, carried 7st (Row). Mr. S. Waldock's br m The Fly, 4yrs, 6st 9lbs (Anderson) ; Mr. A. Clingier's b g New Chum, aged, 6st 7lbs (T. Brown) ; Mr. G. Carmichael's b g Milesian, aged, 6st 7lbs (Tremble) ; Mr. H Fisher's br f Ragpicker, 3yrs, 6st 4lbs, carried 6st 6lbs (S. Davis); Mr. J. Lamb's ch g Cedric, aged, 6st 3lbs, carried 6st 6lbs (Henderson) ; Mr. J. J. Miller's b g Lantern, 6yrs, 6st, carried 6st 11lbs (Lewis).

Betting—5 to 2 agst Tim Whiffler, 3 to 1 Little Fish, 7 to 1 Ragpicker, 9 to 1 Glencoe, 10 to 1 Fly, 15 to 1 Shenandoah, Bylong, Gulnare and Strop, 25 to 50 to 1 others.

Mr. Watson had no slight difficulty in marshalling his five-and-twenty runners in line, the '64 Cup winner, Lantern, playing some pretty circus tricks, thus inducing Shenandoah, never backward at this game, to give trouble also. The flag fell at last to an excellent start, though Booyoolee mistook the direction, and faced round, being left at the post. Barwon and Shenandoah led Little Fish and Mary Anne past the stand in splendid style, the balance being headed by Smolensko, Glencoe, Nimblefoot and Strop, with the favorite well back in the ruck. This order was preserved along the riverside, the Albion pair holding the pride of place, closely followed by Mary Anne. At the back of the course the pace told on Mr. Whitehead's mare, and she retired beaten. Strop here made a forward movement, and Glencoe also came up, the two running third and fourth to Mr. Cleeland's brilliant pair, on whom, however, the pace was beginning to tell, while the favourite, who had bored through his horses, was fifth. Passing the abattoirs, Barwon fell back leaving Glencoe,

M. LARKIN,

AUCTIONEER,

Estate, Insurance and Finance Agent,

200 CLARENDON ST.,

SOUTH MELBOURNE.

LOANS NEGOTIATED TO ANY AMOUNT!

Mortgages Effected on City and Suburban Properties.

City Office - 438 Collins Street (Scott's)

To Squatters, Graziers, Farmers.

NATIONAL

LABOUR EXCHANGE

Supplies the only Reliable Men and Married Couples obtainable.

NO CHARGE TO EMPLOYERS.

SATISFACTION GUARANTEED.

Station Hands, Shearers, Married Couples, Grooms, Gardeners, waiting.

40 LONSDALE ST. EAST,

MELBOURNE.

Trained by owner   **GLENCOE, 1868.**   Ridden by C. Stanley.
Mr John Tait.

Trained by R. Sevior   **WARRIOR, 1869.**   Ridden by J. Murrison
Mr A. Saqui

who had previously cut down Strop, second. Stanley brought the yellow and black forward into the straight, and Strop passed Mr. Cleeland's mare at the distance, her early work now telling severely, but Walsh's gallant efforts were insufficient to land Strop in front of the handsome Glencoe, who won by a good length and a half, amidst very faint cheering, the going down of the favourites having disheartened the public. Three lengths away came Shenandoah, and about the same distance off was the favourite, Tim Whiffler.

Time—3 min. 42 secs.

If the victory of Glencoe proved a surprise, still greater was the astonishment and disgust of the knowing ones at the result of the running in the Melbourne Cup of

1869.

For months previously speculation had been rife, and nearly all of the horses carried large sums of money.

Circassian came to be such a favourite that 2 to 1 was his price at the post, whilst about Traverton fives was the best figure to be got, although he lacked the usual Tait polish.

Notwithstanding the threatening appearance of the morning, the attendance was abnormally large, and this fact was pointed to by the friends of handicaps as a sign of their popularity.

The favourite looked well in his preliminary, but did not extend himself in his usual style.

Although the winner,

Warrior,

a brown gelding, by New Warrior—Annie Laurie, had run very well on the previous Saturday, he was known to have been off his feed on his arrival from Sydney. In those pre-overland days, racehorses had to face the sea voyage, and often got woefully knocked about. It was also known that the owner was starting him against his trainer's wishes. Phœbe looked gross and unfit, whilst Charon, a great lazy colt, evidently wanted more riding than Lewis, who had been wasting, could give him.

The value of the stake was 1240 sovs., being 20 sovs. less than last year.

Mr. A. Saqui's br g WARRIOR, by New Warrior, 6yrs, 8st 10lbs (Morrison) 1
Mr. J. Henderson's br h THE MONK, 5yrs, 7st (W. Enderson) 2
Mr. E. Lee's ch m PHŒBE, 6yrs, 7st 10lbs (S. Davis) 3

Mr. W. Field's b g Strop, aged, 8st 5lbs, carried 8st 7lbs (Haines) ; Mr. D. Melhado's b m Coquette, 4yrs, 8st 4lbs (Waterman) ; Mr. H. J. Bolen's br h Australian, 6yrs, 8st, carried 8st 1½lbs (Yeomans) ; Mr. W. Winch's br h Circassian, 6yrs. 8st, including 5lbs extra (J. Brown) ; Mr. T. Ivory's b g Traverton, aged, 7st 10lbs (Stanley) ; Mr. E. Lee's ch m Barbelle, 4yrs, 7st 8lbs, including 5lbs extra (B. Colley) ; Mr. J. Chaafe's ns br h Sir John, 5yrs, 7st 7lbs (Finn) ; Mr. J. Gilbert's br g Lapdog, 5yrs, 7st 4lbs. carried 7st 8lbs (Munn) ; Mr. J. N. Perkin's ns b g Salem Scudder, aged, 7st 3lbs (Harris) ; Mr. H. Fisher's Albany, 6yrs, 7st 3lbs (D. Mitchell) ; Mr. H. Fisher's b c Charon. 3yrs, 7st (H. Lewis) ; Mr. J. Moffatt's b m Cymba, 4yrs, 6st 12lbs (Master Wilson) ; Mr. G. Lewis's b m Norma, 5yrs, 6st 12lbs (Day) ; Mr. E. T. Barnard's ch g Freetrader, 5yrs, 6st 12lbs (Swales) ; Mr. W. Field's b g Bishopsbourne, 4yrs, 6st 10lbs (T. Enderson); Mr. W. Pearson's b f Kestrel, 3yrs, 6st 7lbs, carried 6st 8½lbs (Davidson) ; Mr. W. J. Clarke's blk h Palmerston, 5yrs, 6st 4lbs (Hubbard) ; Mr. H. Fisher's b m Aurora, 6yrs, 6st 7lbs, including 3lbs extra (Chalker); Mr. J. Kerr's ch h Sheet Anchor, 5yrs, 6st 4lbs (Master Kerr) ; Mr. H. Gamble's br h Paddy's Land, aged, 6st 3lbs (Ward) ; Mr. J. Cain's g m Miranda, aged, 5st 7lbs, carried 5st 11lbs (Bourke) ; Mr. J. Brown's br g Dolo, aged, 5st 7lbs, carried 5st 9lbs (E. Davies) ; Mr. C. Clarke's b m Miss Constance, 4yrs, 5st 7lbs (Master Clarke) also ran.

Betting.—2 to 1 agst Circassian, 5 to 1 Traverton, 6 to 1 Sheet Anchor, 8 to 1 Strop, 10 to 1 Warrior, Charon, Salem Scudder, 100 to 6 Aurora, 100 to 5 Albany and Phœbe, any price others.

The twenty-six horses gave but little trouble, as after one false start they were all got away together.

The cavalcade thundered down the straight in a solid mass, with the exception of Palmerston, who, taking his rider on a voyage of discovery, lost fully 100 yards.

Passing the stand, Bishopsbourne drew out slightly, Traverton being next, in the centre, with Miss Constance for a companion, while Sheet Anchor, pulling double, was on her quarters. Along the river stretch very little change was made, but at the back Warrior came to the front, the favourite being alongside, while Monk, against whom offers of 1000 to 5 had been jeeringly made in the paddock, ran up second at the abattoirs, and Circassian fell back. Then came Sir John, Aurora and Traverton close up, the others tailing off. Before the turn was reached, Traverton cried " enough," while

Warrior led by three lengths into the straight. Morrison took a pull at his horse, allowing Monk to come up a little closer, but the race was all over. Warrior came home an easy winner by a couple of lengths from Monk, whose running into second place was even a greater surprise than Warrior's win. Phœbe, who had been coming very fast, finished third, a length away from Monk.

Time—3min. 40secs.

The following year had an even greater surprise in store, especially for the bookmakers, a large section of whom for once forsook, to a certain extent, their regular business, and backed their fancy to such an extent that after the Cup of

1870

quite a number of the talent had very depleted bank balances. The first to come into prominence was the Duke of Montrose, behind whom the Ballarat dollars were piled. Then he was supplanted by Trump Card, whilst in the meantime Austin Saqui's Warrior was backed so heavily, especially by a certain section of the ring, that the friends of the other favorites, including even the great Tim Whiffler, began to tremble. As the day approached it was found that Lapdog, was heavily backed, and had he won the ring would have suffered even more severely than by Craig's horse,

Nimblefoot,

a bay gelding by Panic—Quickstep. In connection with this race it was stated that the owner of the winner, Mr. Walter Craig, an enthusiastic Ballarat sportsman, had a dream in which he saw the horse Nimblefoot pass the winning-post, the jockey wearing a crape band. Curiously enough when Nimblefoot won, the jockey did wear a crape band, out of respect to the memory of Mr. Craig himself, who died before the race. The authenticity of the dream may be doubtful, but it is certain that J. Slack, one of the ring magnates of the day, paid Mrs. Craig £500 in satisfaction of a bet he had made with her husband on the strength of his dream.

Doubtless the presence of royalty in the shape of the Duke of Edinburgh helped to draw the immense crowd that assembled on this occasion.

The favourites were interviewed, as usual, by great crowds, Warrior, the sensational betting candidate, especially holding an immense levee, and when stripped he looked in perfect condition, as did also Lapdog, although not a taking horse. Trump Card's aristocratic appearance as he came down the straight was the theme of general admiration, whilst Nimblefoot had a strong crowd of friends in consequence of his Saturday's win, when he appropriated the Hotham Handicap.

Value of stake about £1250.

Mr. W. Craig's b g NIMBLEFOOT, by Panic—Quickstep, aged, 6st 3lbs, including 3lbs penalty (Day) ... 1
Mr. J. Gilbert's b g LAPDOG, 6yrs, 7st (Wilson, jur.) 2
Mr. H. Bowler's b g VALENTINE, 3yrs, 6st 4lbs (H. Howard) ... · ... 3

The following also ran :—Mr. E. De Mestre's b h Tim Whiffler, aged, 10st (Donnelly) ; Mr. T. Bailey's ch h Glencoe, 6yrs, 9st 12lbs (Lang); Mr. A. Saqui's b g Warrior, aged, 9st (Morrison) ; Mr. P. Levin's b h Praetor, 5yrs, 8st 4lbs (Yeomans) ; Mr. E. Lee's ch m Barbelle, 5yrs, 8st 4lbs (Colley) ; Mr. J. Tait's ch h The Earl, 5yrs, 8st (Stanley); Mr. J. Cleeland's b g Milesian, aged, 7st 12lbs (T. Enderson) ; Mr. F. Henty's blk h The Monk, 6yrs, 7st 12lbs (Adderley) ; Mr. W. Field's b g Strop, aged, 7st 12lbs (Carter) ; Mr. E. Lee's blk h Barbarian, 4yrs, 7st 10lbs (S. Davis) ; Mr. A. Town's br h Sir William, 5yrs, 7st 9lbs, carried 7st 11lbs (Kean) ; Mr. W. Winch's b c Croydon, 4yrs, 7st 10lbs, including 5lbs penalty (T. Brown) ; Mr. J. Tait's b c The Pearl, 4yrs, 7st 4lbs (H. Lewis); Mr. G. Adams' ch h Trump Card, 5yrs, 7st 5lbs, including 3lbs penalty (Aitkins) ; Mr. J. Chaaffe's ns br h Sir John, aged, 7st 2lbs (Greene); Mr. J. Haines' br h Flying Dutchman, 5yrs, 7st (Bell) ; Mr. E. Lee's b c Partisan, 4yrs, 6st 7lbs (Lemon) ; Mr. J. Brown's b h Duke of Montrose, aged, 6st 9lbs, carried 6st 12½lbs (Rowe) ; Mr. J. Wilson's br m Mischief, 5yrs, 6st 5lbs (Burke) ; Mr. L. Savaraus' ch g Freetrader, 6yrs, 6st 4lbs (Swales); Mr. S. Waldock's ns br h Palmerston, 6yrs, 6st 2lbs (W. Enderson) ; Mr. H. Gamble's br h Paddy's Land, aged, 6st (Sherringham) ; Mr. H. Hett's g g Huntsman, 5yrs, 6st (W. B. Brown) ; Mr. J. E. Crooke's g g Saladin, 6yrs, 5st 10lbs (Ewart) ; Mr. R. J. Harper's br m Patience, 6yrs, 5st 7lbs (Chalker).

Betting.—5 to 1 agst Trump Card, Lapdog and Warrior ; 6 to 1 agst Tim Whiffler ; 8 to 1 agst Glencoe and Croydon ; 12 to 1 agst Barbarian and Nimblefoot; 20 to 25 to 1 agst others.

Of the 72 horses nominated, just 28, or the same number as the Barb's year, faced Mr. Watson, who was lucky enough to get them away at the first attempt. Barbelle's colors were in front by half a length passing

NIMBLEFOOT, 1870.
Mr Walter Craig.

Trained by W. Lang *Ridden by J. Day*

THE PEARL, 1871.
Mr John Tait

Trained by owner *Ridden by Cavanagh*

and subsequently by Romula, who managed to run up to the Pearl, and caused Cavenagh to use the whalebone, when the friendless one gamely responded and beat the mare by a couple of lengths; Irish King a length behind Romula, beating Saladin by half a neck, then came Little Dick fifth, Mermaid sixth, Pyrrhus next, with Cleolite and the Baron next, the rest all over the field.

Time—3min. 39secs.

A protest was entered against Pearl on the ground that Cavenagh struck Romula over the head when passing her. After hearing evidence the protest was dismissed, and the Hillites, especially, cheered loudly when they learnt that Honest John's third Cup victory was safe.

Following up his success, Mr. John Tait scored yet another win in

1872,

when his ever victorious colors were again borne to the front this time by a Tasmanian bred horse,

The Quack,

a dark bay, standing 15 1½in., by Peter Wilkins—Quickstep. Undoubtedly the Fates were kind to the great Sydney sportsman, in that both the second and third horses, though much superior to the winner, were slightly out of form. Dagworth had been a 2 to 1 favorite till his running in the Melbourne Stakes revealed his condition, after which he went back to 100 to 5. That Mr. Tait and his friends understood the state of affairs after this may be gathered from the fact that his commissioner was always prepared to support The Quack at a reasonable price. His example quite animated the public, who, from being so sweet on Dagworth, and Dagworth only, now gave the bookmakers a show, by piling the money on Contessa, King of the Ring, The Ace, and Patriarch, as well as the bearer of the yellow and black. In the saddling paddock there was a generally expressed opinion that Mr. De Mestre had thrown the race away through being too kind to Dagworth. The Ace was much fancied, and impressed one with the idea that if the Sydney sportsmen didn't take our Cup, South Australia would, so anyway we were fair game. It was

noted at the time that of the first five horses finishing in this race, not one was bred in Victoria.

Notwithstanding the intense heat, accompanied by hot wind, there was an immense attendance, estimated at between 40,000 and 50,000. The value of the stake was £1160, being a sweepstakes of 20 sovs. each, with 300 sovs. added.

Mr. J. Tait's b h THE QUACK, by Peter Wilkins—Quickstep, 6yrs, 7st 10lbs. including 8lbs penalty (W. Enderson)   1
Mr. T. J. Ryan's b h THE ACE, by Ace of Clubs—Gwendoline, 4yrs, 8st 4lbs (Hales) 2
Mr. R. Bloomfield's b h DAGWORTH, by Yattendon — Nutcut, 4yrs, 7st 12lbs, including 8lbs penalty (Donnelly) 3

The following also ran :—Mr. E. Lee's ch m Barbelle, aged, 8st 7lbs (Joe Kean); Mr. A. Chirnside's b g The Baron, aged, 8st 1lb. carried 8st 2lbs (McClelland); Mr. P. J. Keighran's ns b g Valentine, aged, 8st 1lb (Sullivan); Mr. J. Tait's ch h The Count, 5yrs, 7st 11bs, including 3lbs penalty (Lewis); Mr. J. J. Miller's ch h Irish King, 4yrs, 8st (Swales); Mr. E. Moran's b h Emblem, 5yrs, 7st 9lbs, carried 7st 11lbs (Corrigan); Mr. A. Saqui's br h Misty Morn, 6yrs 7st 9lbs (Haugh); Mr. A. Chirnside's b m Gironde, 4yrs, 7st 7lbs, carried 7st 8lbs (Rowe); Mr. R. Whitehead's b h Boatman, aged, 7st 4lbs (W. Rees); Mr. W. Filgate's blk m Contessa, 4yrs, 7st 3lbs (J. Sherringham); J. Coldham's b h Early Morn, 5yrs, 7st 4lbs, including 3lbs penalty (J. Wilson); Mr. J. Thompson's b c King of the Ring, 3yrs, 6st 12lbs (W. Wilson); Mr. J. Evans' br c Planter, 5yrs, 6st 10lbs, carried 6st 12lbs (S. Davis); Mr. W. Filgate's b f Dolphin, 4yrs, 6st 4lbs (Grubb); Mr. A. Chirnside's br m Shannon, 4yrs, 6st 4lbs (Chalker); Mr. E. Lee's Patriarch, 3yrs, 6st, carried 6st 2lbs (Cracknell); Mr. J. McFarland's b h Athelstane, 5yrs, 5st 7lbs. carried 5st 9lbs (Robinson); Mr. A. Anderson's ch g Novice (late Alfred). aged, 5st 7lbs, carried 5st 11½lbs (Swannell).

Betting.—4 to 1 agst Contessa; 5 to 1 The Ace; 6 to 1 The Quack; 7 to 1 each King of the Ring and Dagworth; 10 to 1 each Early Morn, Dolphin and Patriarch; 20 to 1 to 50 to 1 others.

King of the Ring and The Ace, the former especially, got very much the worst of a moderate start, in which Valentine, Irish King, The Count and Benjiroo gained the advantage. Down the straight they thundered, Benjiroo making the pace a cracker as he led past the stand, closely followed by The Count, Valentine, Contessa and The Quack in that order, while Dagworth was last, with the exception of King of the Ring, who was far in the rear.

Benjiroo still continued his onward career as the horses rounded

the turn, his nearest attendants being Valentine, The Count, Boatman and Misty Morn. Then The Ace went through his horses and raced with Benjiroo, The Count being just behind the pair, with Misty Morn next, closely followed by Barbelle and The Quack. Dagworth forced his way to the front rank as they passed the abattoirs, and soon after The Count retired, while Benjiroo cried enough at the sheds, leaving The Ace and The Quack at the head of affairs. The Ace had a slight lead as they entered the straight, but Enderson moved on his horse at the distance, and coming away won comfortably by two lengths. Dagworth going under the whip, being defeated for second place by a neck.

Time—3m. 39·5 secs.

We now come to the memorable Cup of

1873,

which was won by the celebrated

Don Juan,

a bay horse by Lucifer—dam Levity. This remarkable horse, nominated by Mr. Johnstone, had been conditionally purchased previous to the race by Mr. Inglis, though actually owned at the time by Mr. Jas. Wilson ; and his winning put so much money in Mr. Joe Thompson's pocket that the latter signalised the victory by the erection of " Don Juan House," a magnificent residence in East Melbourne.

Mr. Wilson was heartily cheered, and received the congratulations of his friends at having broken the spell by gaining first place in this great event, after running second for it no less than three times.

The best performer in the race was undoubtedly Dagworth, who carried 9st 9lbs into second place ; while Horatio showed such pace that had his damaged foot not given way, Don Juan must have travelled even faster to have won.

Lapidist, the Derby hero, and Mr. Tait's pair, McCallum Mohr and The Arrow had hosts of admirers.

It was estimated that over 60,000 people were present, and the crush at Spencer-street was something to be remembered, while one poor fellow was killed at the racecourse platform. As the horses wended their way to the starting-post the scene on the hill, stand and flat was such as had never before been witnessed. The value of the stakes increased this year to 1430 sovs.

Mr. W. Johnstone's b h DON JUAN, by Lucifer—Levity, 4yrs, 6st 12lbs (W. Wilson)... 1
Mr. R. Bloomfield's b h DAGWORTH, 5yrs, 9st 9lbs, including 5lbs penalty (G. Donnelly)... 2
Mr. E. De Mestre's b h HORATIO, 4yrs, 7st 13lbs, including 5lbs penalty (M. Thompson) 3
Mr. J. Crozier's, jur., b h Hamlet, 5yrs, 9st 7lbs (T. Enderson) ; Mr. H. Herbert's b h Priam, 4yrs, 8st 2lbs (G. Thomsen) ; Mr. J. Tait's b h The Arrow, 4yrs, 8st 2lbs (H. Lewis) ; Mr. T. J. Ryan's ch h Lancer, 5yrs, 8st (Hales) ; Mr. S. G. Bowler's b g Exile (late Lapdog), aged, 7st 12lbs (Gardener) ; Mr. W. Pearson's br m Dolphin, 5yrs, 7st 11lbs (Nolan) ; Mr. E. Jellett's ch h King of Clubs, 4yrs, 7st 11lbs (Jellett) ; Mr. J. Tait's b h McCallum Mohr, 6yrs, 7st 9lbs (W. Enderson) ; Mr. J. Coldham's br h Early Morn, 6yrs, 7st 9lbs (Bryan) ; Mr. R. Holland's br h Calaba, 4yrs, 7st 7lbs (Hill) ; Mr. L. P. Winter's b g Protos, 6yrs, 7st 7lbs (Haughey) ; Mr. F. Gough's b g Index, aged, 7st 4lbs (Swannell) ; Mr. W. Gerrard's b h Ace of Trumps, 5yrs, 7st 2lbs (Cracknell) ; Mr. C. S. King's Benjiroo, 5yrs, 6st 10lbs (Chalker) ; Mr. P. Lewis's br h King Tom, 4yrs. 6st 10lbs, carried 6st 12½lbs (S. Davis) ; Mr. W. Filgate's b c Lapidist, 3yrs, 6st 10lbs, carried 6st 11lbs (H. Grubb) ; Mr. K. Brown's br g Victorian, aged, 6st 10lbs (Batty) ; Mr. R. J. Hunter's ch h Lothair, 5yrs, 6st 8lbs (John Kean) ; Mr. A. Chirnside's br g Fearnaught, 4yrs, 6st 8lbs (Ross) ; Mr. E. Jellett's b g Bismarck. aged, 6st 7lbs (Green) ; Sir H. Robinson's b c Fitz-Yattendon, 3yrs, 5st 9lbs, carried 5st 10½lbs (Duggan), also ran.

Betting.—3 to 1 agst Don Juan ; 5 to 1 Horatio ; 6 to 1 Lapidist ; 8 to 1 Fitz-Yattendon ; 10 to 1 The Arrow and Benjiroo ; 15 to 1 each Early Morn, Hamlet and King Tom ; 30 to 50 to 1 others.

Mr. Watson was particularly successful in getting his horses away on even terms, Dagworth being quickest on his legs, though Fitz-Yattendon and The Arrow showed in advance before a hundred yards had been traversed. As they tore past the stand, Protos, Fearnaught and Calaba occupied prominent positions, with The Arrow, Horatio, Dagworth and Fitz-Yattendon on their quarters, Don Juan and Lapidist being close up. At the river side, Protos still led, followed by Hamlet, Early Morn, Priam, Benjiroo, Lothair and Victorian. Don Juan was pulled out on the off side, and after passing his horses one by one, he got on terms with Protos, when the excitement of the multitude became intense as the rank outsider raced on in advance of the favourite. Then Benjiroo became prominent, while Horatio and Dagworth just kept in advance of Hamlet, who was closely attended by Lapidist and Fitz-Yattendon.

At the abattoirs, Don Juan took the lead as Protos fell back beaten, and Dagworth and Horatio came forward, but the latter's "doubtful leg" gave way at this critical moment and he fell back a little. King Tom then made a fruitless effort to get on terms with the leaders, and Fitz-Yattendon and Benjiroo cried a go. At the turn, Lapidist was out of it, and Hamlet breaking down, the issue was left to the three jockies in black. Dagworth came close to Don Juan as they neared the end of the rails, but young Wilson giving the latter a couple of reminders, he shot out in a wonderful manner, was never headed, and won with the greatest ease by three lengths, despite the desperate efforts of Mr. De Mestre's pair, who finished, Dagworth second and Horatio third.

Time—3min. 36secs.

Long before the day Goldsbrough and The Diver were the favourites for the Grand Prix of Australia in

1874.

Prices shortened as the day approached, until threes and fours were the best obtainable about Goldsbrough and King of the Ring, behind whom there were tons of money, whilst about The Diver backers could get 7 and 8 to 1.

The ever increasing popularity of the meeting was well attested by this year's attendance, the number present when the Cup was run for being estimated at fully 75,000.

Of the very numerous Cup candidates, the favourite, Goldsbrough, commanded most attention, his condition and general form being simply perfect. Ashworth, who was to ride him, looked somewhat wasted and weak, but so pleased were the friends of the stable that before starting 2 to 1 was the best obtainable offer. King of the Ring's supporters could find no fault with their favourite's appearance, and his starting price came to 5 to 2. The Diver was in excellent trim, and found many friends, whilst Dagworth was scarce-

ly noticed, and a light bay gelding, standing fully 16 hands high, named

Haricot,

by Lady Kirk—Saucepan, was quite neglected. Value of stake £1210.

Mr. A. Chirnside's b g HARICOT, by Lady Kirk — Saucepan, 6st 7lbs (Pigott) 1
Mr. J. Wilson's b g PROTOS, by Premier —Miss Crawford, aged, 8st 2lbs (G. Arthur) 2
Mr. C. Dublin's br h THE DIVER (late Dolphin), by Maribyrnong—Gwendoline, 4yrs. 6st 10lbs (Greville) ... 3

Mr. E. De Mestre's b h Dagworth, 6yrs, 10st (G. Donnelly); Mr. J. Watts' br m Lurline, 5yrs, 8st 11lbs (R. Mason); Mr. J. Wilson's b h King of the Ring, 5yrs, 8st 7lbs (W. Wilson); Mr. J. Tait's b h Goldsbrough, 4yrs, 8st 5lbs (Ashworth); Mr. J. Tait's b h The Arrow, 5yrs, 8st (Grubb); Mr. W. Filgate's b h Lapidist, 4yrs, 7st 11lbs (J. Day); Sir H. Robinson's b h Fitz-Yattendon, 4yrs, 7st 10lbs (W. Thompson); Mr. J. Brewer's b g After Dark, aged, 7st 8lbs (Watson); Sir H. Robinson's b h Speculation, 4yrs, 7st 6lbs (Duggan); Mr. S. P. Winter's b h Goshawk, 4yrs, 7st 4lbs (Musgrave); Mr. P. Lewis's br h King Tom, 5yrs, 7st (S. Davis); Mr. W. Filgate's br g Gloom, 4yrs, 6st 9lbs (Nolan); Mr. J. Coldham's b h Break o' Day, 5yrs, 6st 5lbs (J. Ryan); Mr. F. Leng's ch h Kettledrum, 4yrs, 6st 4lbs (Cleary); Mr. A. Williamson's b m Cleolite, 4yrs, 5st 12lbs (Scrivener).

Betting.—2 to 1 agst Goldsbrough, 5 to 2 King of the Ring, 6 to 1 The Diver, 7 to 1 Break of Day, 10 to 1 Lurline, The Arrow and Fitz-Yattendon, 16 to 1 Dagworth and Haricot, 20 to 50 to 1 others.

If the assemblage of spectators was abnormally large, the field of horses was unusually small, Mr. Watson only having to face eighteen. He sent them off to an excellent start, The Arrow, Protos and Goldsbrough being on the inside, King Tom, Lapidist and Kettledrum in the centre, whilst on the extreme outside was The Diver. The Arrow was first to show ahead, but passing the stand he was second, Kettledrum leading, and making the pace very hot. The favourite, close behind his stable companion, led Speculation and Haricot from The Diver, whilst Protos headed the balance of the field, which was closely packed, Dagworth and King of the Ring being far behind. The Arrow joined Kettledrum along the river side, whilst Haricot had run up third; then came Goldsbrough, Cleolite, Fitz-Yattendon and The Diver. Near the railway bridge, the neglected Haricot shot to the front, and at the bridge led by a dozen lengths from The Arrow, Diver and Golds-

Fred. Woodhouse. Senr Pinxt.   H. J. Woodhouse, Lith.

Trained by S. Harding   **HARICOT, 1874.**   Ridden by P. Pigott
Messrs T. & A. Chirnside.

Fred. Woodhouse Senr Pinxt,   H. J. Woodhouse, Lith.

Trained by S. Moon   **WOLLOMAI, 1875.**   Ridden by R. Batty
Mr. J. Cleeland

brough. At the abattoirs Haricot was fully twenty lengths ahead of The Diver, who had set sail after him, and who managed to lessen the gap between them by the time the sheds were reached. Entering the straight, it looked as if The Diver would catch Haricot, but Greville was too weak to make the most of his mount, and a hundred yards from home he was headed by Protos, who beat him by a neck for second place, the pair being unable to get on terms with Haricot, who won easily by four lengths. From the time Haricot took command the race was simply a run-away, such as had never been witnessed on Flemington since Archer galloped over his field.

Time—3min. 37secs.

After gladdening the hearts of the Messrs. Chirnside, Dame Fortune now smiled on Mr. John Cleeland, whose many disappointments so well deserved to be crowned with success. As a reward for his perseverance, the host of the Albion was greeted in

1875

with the cheers of a multitude far greater than that which attended the Cup when his speedy grey ran into third place seven years before.

The victory of

Wollomai,

by Ace of Clubs—Fleur de Lis, was witnessed by an enormous attendance.

In the saddling paddock, the horse most sought after was Imperial, and as Messrs. De Mestre and Cox were confident, the money was piled on, even when 3 to 1 was the best offer against him.

The winner, a light bay horse, was bred and owned by Mr. Cleeland, who nominated under the assumed name of Mr. Sharp, and although it had been generally asserted that Wollomai was not in the race, " Augur," in *The Australasian*, had always maintained that he had done more genuine work than any other horse at Flemington.

Imperial, Kingsborough, Kingfisher, Goldsbrough, Richmond, Dilke, and others, were scanned eagerly, while Wollomai was treated with something of the disdain that was accorded Haricot in the previous year.

Mr. H. Sharp's b h WOLLOMAI, by Ace of Clubs, 6yrs. 7st 8lbs (Batty)   1
Mr. E. Jellett's br c RICHMOND, 3yrs, 6st 3lbs (Williams) 2
Mr. J. Tait's b h GOLDSBROUGH, 5yrs, 9st 9lbs (Ashworth) 3
Mr. J. B. Wallis's ch m Calumny, 6yrs, 9st 3lbs (H. Lewis); Sir H. Robinson's b h Kingsborough, 4yrs, 8st 11lbs (W. Yeomans); Mr. T. Ivory's b h Sterling, 5yrs, 8st 7lbs (M. Bryan); Mr. J. Tait's b h Melbourne, 4yrs, 8st 6lbs (Grubb); Mr. A. S. Cox's ch g Imperial, 6yrs, 8st 4lbs (J. Morrison); Messrs. T. and A. Chirnside's b g Haricot. 5yrs 8st 2lbs (Lynch); Mr. G. Livingstone's b h Scanmag, 4yrs, 7st 12lbs (J. McInnes); Messrs. T. and A. Chirnside's b g Nimrod, 6yrs. 7st 2lbs (Green); Mr. S. Waldock's br h Calaba, 6yrs. 6st 12lbs (Snarey); Mr. Matthews' br h West Australian, 5yrs, 6st 10lbs (Cleary); Mr. W. McKenzie's blk m Coquette, 4yrs, 6st 7lbs (W. Howard); Mr. J. E. Warby's b or br h Polidori, 4yrs, 6st 4lbs (Hummerstone); Mr. A. Cornwell's ch g Kingfisher, aged, 6st 4lbs (Ridley); Mr. G. Atkinson's br h Dilke. 4yrs, 6st 2lbs (S. Cracknell); Mr. S. P. Winter's b g Mohican, 4yrs, 6st 2lbs (Harden); Mr. D. McLellan's b m Kincrachnie, 6yrs, 6st 13lbs (W. McLeod); Mr. G. Bennett's br f Loquacity, 3yrs, 5st 9lbs (Fitzpatrick).

Betting.—3 to 1 agst Imperial, 5 to 1 Kingsborough, 7 to 1 Kingfisher, 10 to 1 each Goldsbrough and Dilke, 12 to 1 Haricot, 18 to 1 each Wollomai, Richmond and Sterling, 20 to 30 to 1 others.

The horses eventually got off on excellent terms, Goldsbrough, Nimrod, Mohican, Kingsborough and Coquette showing prominently on the right, Dilke in the rear, and losing ground at every stride.

Passing the stand, Polidori led, Nimrod second, Coquette third, Mohican fourth, with Goldsbrough, Kingsborough, Richmond, Haricot and others close together; Dilke twenty lengths in the rear. Nimrod gained a momentary advantage at the turn, but bolted inside, and Polidori resumed the lead at a rattling pace, Coquette second, followed by Kincrachnie and Mohican side by side. The pace began to tell on Polidori and he gave way to Coquette; then Kincrachnie took second place, Goldsbrough third, Mohican, Kingsborough and Imperial next, in that order; while Wollomai was in a good position on the outside, with Richmond and Loquacity close at his heels. Wollomai, improving his position, was nearly on terms with Coquette at the sheds. The horses were in a cluster, and as they made the last turn, Coquette was slightly ahead, Wollomai at her girths, Richmond with his neck between the latter and Goldsbrough. Wollomai supplanted Coquette, and stalled off Goldsbrough's rush, but was immediately after joined by Richmond, and an exciting struggle took place for a few strides, when the little horse began to roll with his tiny rider, and amidst tremendous shouting Wollomai drew away inside the distance, and won rather easily by two lengths. Goldsbrough third, four lengths behind Richmond.

Time—3min. 38secs.

The following year indeed was a surprise, as for the first time since the institution of the Cup race, it was won by a mare in

1876.

The St. Albans stable had the honor of furnishing the successful candidate, although in winning the big event,

Briseis,

had to cut down her heavily-backed stable companion, Feu d'Artifice. A few knowing ones, however, put their pile on the filly Briseis. Timothy, Irish Stew and Aldinga had also numerous friends.

About 75,000 people were present.

Value of stakes £1850, being a sweepstakes of 20 sovs each with 500 added, and a gold cup presented by Mr. James Blackwood.

Mr. J. Wilson's br f BRISEIS, by Tim Whiffler (imp.)—Musidora, 3yrs, 6st 4lbs (St. Albans) 1

Mr. R. Sevior's br f SIBYL, by Tim Whiffler (imp.)—Jessica, 3yrs, 6st (Phelps) 2

Mr. E. De Mestre's b h TIMOTHY, by Tim Whiffler (Sydney)—Lady, 4yrs, 7st (Nicholson) 3

Mr. W. S. Cox's ch g Imperial, aged, 8st 10lbs (W. Yeomans); Messrs. T. and A. Chirnside's b h Sultan, 6yrs, 8st 6lbs (T. Wilson); Mr. T. Levy's b m Southern Cross, 5yrs, 8st 6lbs (Kavenagh); Mr. T. Ivory's b h Sterling, 5yrs, 8st 6lbs (Colley); Sir H. Robinson's b h Clifton, late Richmond, 4yrs, 8st (Ramsay); Mr. J. Cleeland's b h Dilke, 5yrs, 7st 10lbs (R. Batty); Mr. W. Yuille, jr., ns b g Mountaineer, 6yrs, 7st 9lbs (Huey); Mr. G. Bennett's b h Emulation, 4yrs, 7st 8lbs (Murphy); Mr. G. Bennett's bl h Impudence, 4yrs, 7st 7lbs (W. Enderson); Mr. H. Power's b m Feu d'Artifice, 5yrs, 7st 5lbs (T. Hales); Mr. J. J. Miller's ch h Janitor, 4yrs, 7st 4lbs (Willis); Mr. J. Arthur's br h Spark, 4yrs, 6st 12lbs (E. Bancroft); Mr. J. Crozier, junior's b m Venus, 6yrs, 6st 12lbs (Aspinall); Mr. C. B. Fisher's br m Onyx, 4yrs, 6st 10lbs (Ivemy); Messrs. T. and A. Chirnside's br g Nunnykirk 4yrs, 6st 8lbs (Hood); Mr. W. Yuille, jr., ns b h Torchlight, 5yrs, 6st 8lbs (S. Davis); Mr. W. Field's br m Bella, 4yrs, 6st 8lbs (W. Motton jr.); Mr. Keighran's b h Fisherman, 4yrs, 6st 8lbs (Power); Mr. J. J. Miller's b or br g Irish Stew, 4yrs, 6st 8lbs (Pigott) Mr. J. Hill's b g Vain Hope, aged, 6st 8lbs (Nolan);

Mr. A. Bowman's b m Kismet, 4yrs, 6st 6lbs (Hinks); Mr. L. Barnard's g g The Deer. aged, 6st 4lbs (Snarey); Mr. R. T. Reid's b c Pride of the Hills, 3yrs, 6st 4lbs (Spooner); Mr. R. Holland's blk c Electricity. 3yrs, 6st 1lb (Thompson); Mr. S. Gardiner's b or br c Aldinga, 3yrs, 6st (Williams); Mr. L. L. Smith's g c Glengarry, 3yrs, 5st 10lbs (King); Mr. W. S. Cox's b c Spring Jock, aged, 5st 7lbs (Taylor); Mr. E. Hunt's b g Disraeli. aged, 5st 7lbs (Braithwaite); Mr. D. D. Simpson's br f Gentility, 3yrs, 5st 7lbs (Enwright); Mr. J. Paterson's br f, 3yrs, 5st 7lbs (Heywood).

Betting—4 to 1 Feu d'Artifice, 6 to 1 Briseis, 8 to 1 Timothy, 10 to 1 Spark and Irish Stew, 13 to 1 Aldinga, 20 to 30 to 1 others.

The largest field that had ever started for a Melbourne Cup faced Mr. Watson, there being 32 horses on the line. That gentleman was, however, fortunate to get them away at first call to a splendid start. The pace up the straight was very fast, Aldinga holding a good lead, which he maintained past the stand, Sultan, Torchlight, Imperial and Clifton being his close companions. Feu d'Artifice was in a good position in the centre of the second flight passing the stand, with Irish Stew on the outside, while Briseis and Sibyl were next the rails. The cheers seemed to madden Sultan, who getting out of control rushed past Aldinga and led to the turn, where, however, Aldinga again led, and made the pace a cracker along the river side, where Spring Jock, who had been brought forward at a terrible rate, took command. Irish Stew was now second, having stolen in from the rails, whilst Timothy, who had threaded his horses cleverly, was fourth on Aldinga's quarters. Nearing the bridge, Impudence, Sterling and Emulation secured forward places, the pace being still very hot. Passing the sheds Spring Jock had a slight lead from Impudence and Timothy, whilst Sibyl, Irish Stew, Emulation and Imperial were close by, with Briseis coming up fast. Irish Stew was in front half a mile from home, a length away from Spring Jock; but both cried enough at the turn, and Sibyl forged ahead, obtaining a lead into the straight of a couple of lengths from Impudence, who was in trouble, whilst Irish Stew on the outside was under the whip. Briseis, who was comparatively fresh, bored her way through, and cutting down Sibyl in front of the stand, won by a length

THOMAS BYRNE,

WARRNAMBOOL HOTEL,

436 BOURKE STREET WEST, MELBOURNE.

First-Class Wines and Spirits.

✠ STORK ✠ HOTEL, ✠

ELIZABETH STREET.

PRICE MEREDITH - - Proprietor

(Son of the late T. Meredith, Chewton).

The Union Finance Guarantee & Investment Co.

OF AUSTRALIA, LIMITED,

UNION CHAMBERS, 30 LITTLE COLLINS ST. WEST.

SUBSCRIBED CAPITAL, A QUARTER OF A MILLION.

Directors:

ALFRED SHAW, ESQ., Chairman.   HON. ALFRED DEAKIN, M.P.   ROBERT REID, ESQ.
WILLIAM M'LEAN, ESQ., J.P.   CHARLES SMITH, ESQ., M.P.

This Company is prepared to Finance and Guarantee, Discount Bills of Exchange, Advance on Merchandise and other Securities, Float Companies under the Limited Liability Act, and to transact Financial and Agency Business generally.

THOMAS PARSONS, General Manager.

The Colonial Mutual Life Assurance Society,

LIMITED.

Branches throughout the Colonies and the United Kingdom.

Policies Issued under the ORDINARY, MODIFIED TONTINE and MORTUARY DIVIDEND System.

ANNUAL INCOME EXCEEDS £300,000.

New Business for the Past Five Years Exceeds 6½ Millions.

Premiums are Moderate and Policies Entirely Free from Restrictions or Harassing Conditions.

Trained by owner

BRISEIS, 1876
Mr. J. Wilson

Ridden by P. St Albans

Trained by E. De Mestre

CHESTER 1877.
Hon. J. White

Ridden by P. Pigott

and a half amid tumultuous cheering, the determined manner in which St. Albans sat down and brought his mount home, having fairly won the race. A length from Sibyl came Timothy, who secured third place.

Time—3min. 36¼sec.

The Cup of the following year was memorable for two special circumstances; first, that in

1877

the Hon. James White began that career on the Australian turf which has hitherto been unparalleled, and which it is hoped will culminate in his winning, if not the English Derby, some of the big events. The second notable circumstance was that the winner,

Chester,

a handsome son of Yattendon, out of Lady Chester, like Briseis in the year previous, pulled off the coveted double—Derby and Cup.

Chester was strongly backed early in the season at fairly long odds; but after his Derby win his price became very short, and he went out at 5 to 1. The St. Albans people having pinned their faith to Savanaka, his price shortened rapidly, and those who had laid long odds against him early in the betting, being anxious to save themselves, there was so much in the market on his behalf, that he took the pride of place at 4 to 1. The deceitful Painter had many friends, whilst on the other hand Newminster, once a strong favorite, was now unnoticed.

Fortunately the rain held over until the afternoon, and 90,000 people swarmed out to see the great race.

Value of stakes £1940, a sweepstakes of 20 sovs. each, with £500 added.

Hon. J. White's b c CHESTER, by Yattendon — Lady Chester, 3yrs, 6st 12lbs (P. Pigott) 1

Mr. H. Power's blk or g c SAVANAKA, by Kingston—Sappho, 3yrs, 6st 2lbs (St. Albans) 2

Mr. G. W. Petty's ch h THE VAGABOND, by Fireworks — Skittle Sharper, 4yrs, 7st (Ivemy) 3

Mr. C. M. Lloyd's br h The Diver, aged, 9st 2lbs (W. Higginbotham); Mr. R. J. Reid's br h Pride of the Hills, 4yrs, 9st (J. Jenkins) ; Mr. J. Cleeland's br h Wollomai, aged, 8st 11lbs (R. Batty) ; Mr. C. B. Fisher's br h Robinson Crusoe, 4yrs, 8st 10lbs (J. Morrison) ; Mr. W. S. Cox's ch g Imperial, aged, 8st 5lbs (D. Sullivan); Mr. J. Mayo's ch h Janitor, 5yrs, 8st 4lbs (B. Colley) ; Mr. A. Chirnside's br h Newminster, 4yrs, 8st 3lbs (W. Yeomans) ; Mr. A. S. Hill's ch g Kingfisher, aged, 8st 1lb (Huxley); Mr. C. B. Fisher's br h The Painter, 5yrs, 8st (S. Davis) ; Mr. H. Phillips' b m Adelaide, 4yrs, 8st (W. Huey) ; Mr. S. Gardiner's br h Aldinga, 5yrs, 7st 10lbs (T. Hales); Mr. W. S. Cox's b g Haricot, aged, 7st 7lbs (M'Innis) ; Mr. W. Mackenzie's br m Coquette, 6yrs, 7st 4lbs (Harrison) ; Mr. C. James' b or br g Tom Kirk, 6yrs, 7st 4lbs (Mascall) ; Mr. E. Jellet's b h Filibuster, 4yrs. 7st 2lbs (Murphy) ; Mr. W. S. Cox's ch h The King, 5yrs, 7st 2lbs (Heywood) ; Mr. Wilson's b g Artful Joe, 5yrs, 6st 12lbs (Joe Wilson) ; Mr. Grant's br h Fisherman, 5yrs, 6st 12lbs (Power) ; Mr. Jordan's Lockleys, 3yrs, 6st 11lbs (Nicholson) ; Mr. Mahon's b m Peerless, 5yrs, 6st 9lbs (King) ; Dr. Bathe's ch h Ralph Leigh, 4yrs, 6st 9lbs (M'Loughlin) ; Mr. H. J. Bowler's ch c Waterford, 3yrs, 6st 9lbs (T. Aspinall) ; Mr. C. Edwards' ch c Royalty, 3yrs, 6st 7lbs (Braithwaite) ; Mr. A. Smith's b g Lord Harry, 6yrs, 6st 6lbs (Nolan) ; Mr. Rounsevell's b f Device, 5yrs, 6st 3lbs (Kilduff) ; Mr. Henty's b h Waxy, 6yrs, 6st 2lbs (Jerrard) ; Mr. Phillips' b c Pluto, 3yrs, 6st (Williamson) ; Mr. Filgate's b c Glenormiston, 3yrs, 5st 12lbs (G. Williams) ; Mr. Tait's br c Amendment. 3yrs, 5st 12lbs (J. Williams) ; Mr. Silberberg's br c Woodlands, 3yrs, 5st 7lbs (Connor).

Betting : 4 to 1 Savanaka, 5 to 1 Chester, 8 to 1 Woodlands and Aldinga, 12 to 1 Painter and Robinson Crusoe, 14 to 1 Haricot, 16 to 1 The Vagabond, Tom Kirk and Pluto. 20 to 25 to 1 others.

The weather had cleared up a little as Mr. Watson got his field away to a moderate start, although Robinson Crusoe and Amendment, colliding as the word was given, were left twenty lengths behind the others. Nearing the distance post Fisherman took the lead and passed the stand a length away from Tom Kirk, Savanaka, Adelaide and Aldinga. Waxy, Peerless, Glenormiston and Chester were in good positions close to Aldinga, whilst Device and Waterford drove the ruck before them. The unfortunate Robinson Crusoe was pounding along many lengths behind everything. Fisherman led at a great pace round the turn, where Waxy was second, the favorite third, and Ralph Leigh next, Tom Kirk and Filibuster followed, while close by was Aldinga running very unkindly, with Chester at his girths and going strongly. At the bridge Fisherman still led at a hot pace, Tom Kirk, Filibuster and Savanaka following in the order named. Waxy and Tom Kirk joined Fisherman at the abattoirs, but the former fell near the sheds, and nearly brought Savanaka down, "Little Dumple" losing a couple of lengths by the mishap. Glenormiston and The Vagabond came forward, the former taking the place of Fisherman in the van. Chester, who was being brought up on the inside, slipped at the turn, but recovered himself quickly and took the straight abreast of Tom Kirk and Woodlands, who were in the centre, Savanaka being on the outside, while Glenormiston held a clear lead from The Vagabond. Pigott called on his horse, who quickly passed The Vagabond and Glenormiston, and being now fairly in front with the race well in hand apparently left off riding, only to find Savanaka coming up with a terrific rush. The excitement amongst the spectators was intense, and as Chester, having been brought again, was landed home half a head in front of Savanaka, the cheering was tremendous. The Vagabond came third, three lengths behind the leaders, Glenormiston fourth, Woodlands fifth.

Time—3min. 33½secs.

The luck of New South Wales in 1877 was not broken in

1878

when surely enough the mother colony was again to the fore. This time Mr. De Mestre, carried off the coveted prize with

Calamia,

who, having been sent back in the betting by Melita and Firebell, started at 10 to 1, there being, however, large sums of money depending on his pushing his handsome head first past the post.

Firebell was persistently put forward as a moral certainty, he having done a big gallop in private, but Melita remained first favorite, and went out at 4 to 1.

In the paddock Melita was greatly admired, as was also Calamia who had many friends, despite the sum on the favorites. Waxy, although somewhat light on the ribs, was big and muscular about the quarters. Considerable attention was drawn to Chester, whose backers were this time doomed to grievous disappointment.

Value of stakes, £1860, being a sweepstakes of 20 sovs., with 500 sovs. added.

Mr. E. De Mestre's b h CALAMIA, by Maribyrnong—Luna, 5yrs, 8st 2lbs (T. Brown) 1
Mr. C. James's br h TOM KIRK, by Ladykirk — Spa, aged, 7st 8lbs (Murphy) 2
Mr. J. L. Purves' br g WAXY, by Croagh Patrick — Leila, 6yrs, 6st 11lbs (Braithwaite) 3

Mr. J. White's b h Chester, 4yrs, 9st (J. Morrison) ; Mr. G. Hill's br h Cap-a-pie, 4yrs, 8st 8lbs (W. Huxley) ; Mr. A. Chirnside's br h Newminster, 5yrs, 8st 8lbs (B. Colley) ; Mr. T. Ivory's br g Macaroni, 6yrs, 8st 6lbs (P. Pigott) ; Mr. T. Jordan's br h Lockleys, 4yrs, 8st 5lbs (J. Kilduff) ; Mr. C. M. Lloyd's b h Swiveller, 4yrs, 7st 13lbs (W. Yeomans) ; Mr. W. Filgate's br h Glenormiston, 4yrs, 7st 12lbs (G. Williams) ; Mr. J. Tait's br h Strathearn, 4yrs, 7st 12lbs (Gordon) ; Mr. W. Brown's blk h Rapidity, 4yrs, 7st 5lbs (Weston) ; Mr. W. Pile's br m Device, 4yrs, 7st 5lbs (T. Hales) ; Mr. S. Bradbury's b g Burwood, aged, 7st 4lbs (S. Davis) ; Mr. S. A. Johnson-Boe's ch h Columbus, 6yrs, 7st 3lbs (T. Aspinall) ; Mr J. Thompson's blk h Devilshoof, 4yrs, 7st 2lbs (Pearson) ; Mr. W. S. Cox's c h The King, 6yrs, 6st 10lbs (W. S. Cox, jr.) : Mr. S. Mahon's br c Franciscan, 3yrs, 6st 8lbs (Deasy) ; Mr. J. Paterson's ch c Warlock, 3yrs, 6st 7lbs (Walker) ; Sir H. Robinson's g f Emily, 3yrs, 6st 6lbs (Williamson) ; Mr. W. Rawlinson's br h Darriwell, 4yrs, 6st 6lbs (S. Cracknell) ; Mr. L. L. Smith's g h Glengarry, 5yrs, 6st 6lbs (Nicholson) ; Mr. A. E. Cornwell's br h Auckland, 4yrs, 6st 5lbs (Cornwell) ; Mr. R. T. Reid's blk f Pride of the Vale, 3yrs, 6st (Gaghan) ; Mr. J. Whittingham's b c Riverton, 3yrs, 5st 12lbs (C. Hutchins) ; Mr. J. Tait's blk c K.C.B., 3yrs, 5st 10lbs (Emsworth) ; Mr. E. A. Johnson-Boe's br c Wellington, 3yrs, 5st 13lbs (J. King) ; Mr. C. G. Baldock's ch g Numa Pompilius, 4yrs, 5st 7lbs (G. Poole) ; Mr. H. J. Bowler's ch f Melita, 3yrs, 5st 7lbs (P. St. Albans) ; Mr. W. S. Cox's ch h Firebell, 4yrs, 5st 7lbs (G. Burton).

Betting—100 to 25 Melita, 100 to 12 Wellington and Firebell, 100 to 10 Calamia, 100 to 8 Chester and Auckland, 100 to 6 Waxy, Columbus, and Emily, 100 to 5 Macaroni, 100 to 4 to 100 to 2 others.

The score and a half of gallant horses that turned their honest faces towards Mr. Watson showed none of the usual fractiousness, whilst the riders emulating their steeds forbore for once to try the usual little tricks which so often resulted in fines from the stern old general in front. Consequently the cavalcade was got off to a good start, Rapidity being the first to show forward, and he led up past the stand, followed by Wellington, Tom Kirk and Chester, with Glengarry, Calamia and Firebell close up.

Trained by owner   **CALAMIA, 1878.**   *Ridden. by T. Brown*
Mr. De Mestre

Trained by W. E. Dakin   **DARRIWELL, 1879.**   *Ridden by S. Cracknell.*
Mr. W. Rawlinson

Columbus, who had had a little difficulty with the " Cup dog," acted as whipper-in, driving along Swiveller, Device, and Pride of the Vale. The order was practically unchanged up to the mile and a quarter post, except that Waxy joined the leaders, when a lamentable accident occurred. Glengarry collided with Tom Kirk and Chester. The latter being on the inside, crushed Morrison against a post, causing him to fall off. Chester then joined the other horses, whilst Glengarry ran inside the course.

Rapidity still led, Waxy and Tom Kirk keeping him at it, whilst close at their heels came Calamia well within himself, and before the abattoirs was passed the race was virtually his, as he ran easily into second place, and half a mile from home passed Rapidity, who fell back beaten. Waxy and Tom Kirk made a gallant struggle to catch the Terara crack, but failed, Calamia winning easily by two lengths and a half from Waxy; whilst a length away Tom Kirk took third place.

Time—3min. 35¾secs.

On being brought in Morrison, who in the first Cup race, 17 years before, had the ill luck to fracture his left arm, was found to have split the bone of his right leg. He never fairly recovered from this accident, and suffered such pain that a few months ago, nearly 11 years after, he was induced to have the leg re-broken and properly set. The operation was too much for him, and he died shortly afterwards.

Suwarrow's brilliant Derby victory on the previous Saturday made him favorite in the betting for the Cup of

1879,

he having supplanted Secundus and Savanaka in the market. The touts were vastly pleased with the performances of Sweetmeat, Lord Harry and Savanaka on the track, the first-named being considered a pretty sure thing by the knowing crowd following Ivory's stable.

Darriwell

Tim Whiffler — Norma, showed great form in a go he had with Le Loup, and was thought very formidable by the Sweetmeat people, Mr. Ivory himself backing him to win a good round sum. It was however supposed that Darriwell could not stay, although Mr. Dakin who, according to his usual practice, concealed nothing respecting his horses, considered he had a fair show.

When the Cup competitors stripped in the paddock, Secundus attracted most attention, and next to him Suwarrow and Savanaka, all three being in splendid condition. Darriwell looked trained to the minute, and those who having watched the good work he had put in, had backed him at a long figure felt comfortable over their wagers. Singularly enough his name appeared as being scratched when the bell-tower list was first exhibited, and many of the superstitious looked upon this as a good omen.

Value of stakes, £1945, being a sweepstakes of 20 sovs. each, with 500 added.

Mr. W. Rawlinson's br h DARRIWELL, by Tim Whiffler (imp.)—Norma, 5yrs, 7st 4lbs (S. Cracknell) 1
Mr. T. Ivory's b h SWEETMEAT, by Yattendon—Sultana, 4yrs, 7st 1lbs (Nicholson) 2
Mr. R. Howie's gr c SUWARROW, by Snowden – Phizgig, 3yrs, 6st 3lbs (G. Williams) 3

Mr. E. Jellett's b h Richmond, aged, 9st 5lbs (Walker); Mr. H. Power's g h Savanaka, 5yrs, 9st 3lbs (T. Hales); Mr. G. Fraser's c h Le Loup, 5yrs, 8st 4lbs (W. Yeomans); Mr. J. White's b h Democrat, 6yrs, 8st 2lbs (Gordon); Mr. E. A. Johnson-Boe's br h Wellington, 4rs, 8st 2lbs (Murphy); Mr. J. Tait's br h Strathearn, 5yrs, 7st 8lbs (S. Davis); Mr. W. Frederick's br g Tom Kirk, aged, 7st 7lbs (J. King); Mr. A. Davies b h Levant, 5yrs, 7st 7lbs (Braithwaite); E. A. Johnson-Boe's ch h Columbus, aged 7st 7lbs (Barr); Mr. W. Filgate's b h Glenormiston, 5yrs, 7st 3lbs (J. Williamson); Mr. F. Leng's b h Monarque, 4yrs, 6st 12lbs (J. Williams); Mr. J. Tait's blk h K.C.B., 4yrs, 6st 7lbs (Deasy); Mr. A. Forrester's ch m Colima, 5yrs, 6st 12lbs (Roarty); Mr. J. L. Purves Waxy, aged, 6st 6lbs (Kelly); Mr. S. Mahon's br h Tidal Wave, 4yrs, 6st 4lbs (Vochler); Mr. Donnelly's br c Falmouth, 3yrs, 6st 4lbs (Gainsford); Mr. J. Whittingham's b h Riverton, 4yrs, 6st 3lbs (J. Kilduff); Mr. J. Mayo's ch h Secundus (late Highlander), 4yrs, 6st 7lbs (O'Connor); Mr. S. Mahon's b h Roland, 4yrs, 6st (Burton); Mr. J. M'Phail's b c Terrific, 3yrs, 5st 12lbs (Greville); Mr. E. De Mestre's b c Caractus, 3yrs, 5st 12lbs (G. Riley); Mr. J. E. Saville's b c The Wandering Jew, 3yrs, 6st (Geoghegan); Mr. G. Livingston's b c Pollio, 3yrs, 5st 7lbs (Fallon).

K.C.B. was first to move, the lot getting away at the first signal; but entering the rails Suwarrow led from Tom Kirk, Riverton and Wellington, and keeping his position right along led past the stand at a terrific pace, while a length behind him Tom Kirk, Monarque, and Riverton raced side by side. Savanaka, who already felt the pace, was with Darriwell, Strathearn, Democrat and Sweetmeat close by, but both he and Richmond unmistakably cut it at the river turn, where Suwarrow still led his field with undiminished speed. Riverton was now next the gallant grey, Wellington third, all three going splendidly, while close up were Calamia, Tom Kirk, and Monarque. Then came a little cluster consisting of Glenormiston, Darriwell, Sweetmeat, and Secundus. Along the back the order of the leaders was unchanged, but Waxy ran up fourth, whilst Calamia, Sweetmeat and Darriwell had moved forward into good positions. Riverton flattered his friends by joining Suwarrow for a hundred yards at the abattoirs, but he soon cried enough, and rounding the turn, left Wellington to look after Suwarrow. Darriwell, who was going well within himself, was next on the inside, and then came Waxy and Sweetmeat. Cracknell, who had hitherto been sitting still on Darriwell, called on him at the distance post, and racing home won cleverly by half a length from Sweetmeat, who, after cutting down Waxy and Colima, beat Suwarrow for second place by a head. Columbus was fourth, Wellington fifth, Colima sixth.

Time—3min. 30¾ secs.

The memory of the Spring Meeting of the following year,

1880

will long live amongst sporting men if only for the turn of speed shown by the brilliant equine wonder,

Grand Flaneur.

Being Exhibition year, the course was crowded with visitors from every part of Australia, New Zealand, and nearly every civilised country under the sun. To find fully a hundred thousand people massed together in an orderly crowd to witness a contest between some of the finest horses in the world, was certainly a surprise to many visitors, especially when they remembered the country had not yet been settled half a century. The various favorites were as usual surrounded by admirers. Mata, about whose doings in the land of the moa so much had been said and written, especially attracting attention. Progress, Grand Flaneur, and Lord Burleigh were in grand fettle, and so strong was the support accorded them that they supplanted Mata in the betting.

Value of stake, £1785, being a sweepstakes of 20 sovs. each, with 500 sovs. added.

Mr. W. A. Long's GRAND FLANEUR, by Yattendon—First Lady, 3yrs, 6st 10lbs (T. Hales) 1
Mr. W. Branch's PROGRESS, by Angler —Coquette, 3yrs, 5st 10lbs (St. Albans) 2
Mr. F. N. L. Rossi's br h Lord Burleigh, by Yattendon — Lady Constance, 5yrs, 7st 5lbs (Pigott)... 3

Hon. J. White's br h Chester 6yrs, 9st 6lbs (Huxley) ; Mr. T. Jones's br h Woodlands 6yrs, 8st 10lbs (J. King); Mr. E. Jellet's br h Bosworth, 5 yrs, 8st 8lbs (Walker); Sir T. Elder's br h Darriwell, 6yrs, 8st 7lbs (M. O'Brien) ; Hon. J. White's b h Martindale, 6yrs, 8st 7lbs (Gordon) ; Mr. H. Vallance's b g Mata, 6yrs, 8st 2lbs (Clifford); Mr. W. Pile's ch c First Water, 4yrs, 8st 1lb (Campbell); Mr. C. L. MacDonald's b g Banter, aged, 7st 13lbs (Gaghan); Mr. E. Jellet's br h Richmond, aged, 7st 12lbs (Barlow); Mr. T. Jordan's b f Rivalry, 4yrs, 7st 8lbs (W. Murphy) ; Mr. J. Mayo's ch h Secundus, 5yrs, 7st 10lbs (Roarty); Mr. W. H. Kent's Napper Tandy, 5yrs, 7st 1lb (Williamson); Mr. J. Whittingham's b h Riverton 5yrs, 7st (Burton); Mr. J. E. Savill's br h The Wandering Jew, 4yrs, 7st (J. Kilduff) ; Mr. J. Mayo's ch c Elastic, 4yrs, 6st 13lbs (Emsworth) ; Mr. K. Warn's b h Auckland, 6yrs, 6st 8lbs (Nicholson); Mr. W. Pile's b or br c Rothschild, (Curr); Mr. Howie's b c Lothair, 3yrs, 6st (Cracknell) ; Mr. J. H. Hill's br c Totalisator, 3yrs, 5st 9lbs (Bowes).

Betting: 2 to 1 agst Progress, 4 to 1 Lord Burleigh and Grand Flaneur, 7 to 1 Mata, 12 to 1 Darriwell, Auckland and Napper Tandy. 16 to 25 to 1 others.

Lothair was troublesome at the post, kicking Darriwell in the shoulder, but at last Mr. Watson got his field of 22 away safely. Mata, who was on the inside, Totalisator, Elastic, Lothair, Progress and Grand Flaneur were first to move. Elastic's colors showed in front for a few lengths, when Napper Tandy took command and brought the cavalcade right up the straight at a moderate pace, but passing the stand Lothair was in front, with Totalisator and Napper Tandy at his girths, and then followed Progress, Auckland, Woodlands, Riverton, and Grand Flaneur,

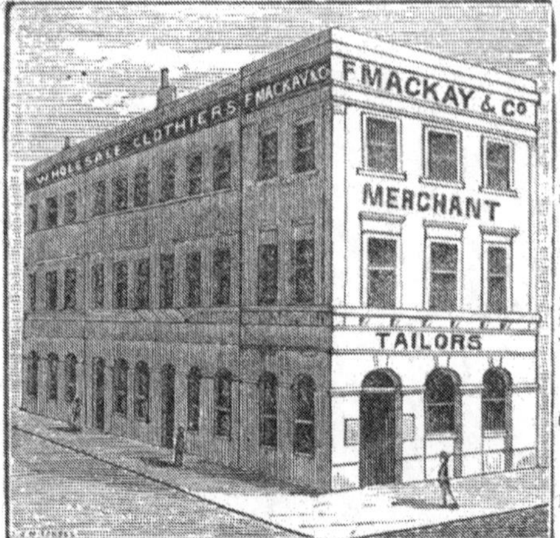

V.A.T.C. RACING FIXTURES.

1889-90.

DATE OF RUNNING.			NOMINATIONS CLOSE.
Saturday. 17th August, 1889 ...	...	...	29th July.
Saturday, 14th September, 1889	...	...	2nd September.
Saturday, 12th October, 1889			
Saturday, 19th October, 1889	...	...	23rd September.
Thursday, 26th December, 1889	...	...	9th December.
Saturday, 25th January, 1890	...	...	6th January.
Saturday, 22nd February, 1890	...	...	3rd February.
Saturday, 22nd March, 1890 ...	..	...	3rd March.
Saturday, 5th April, 1890	...	...	24th March.
Saturday, 3rd May, 1890	...	...	21st April.
Saturday, 28th June, 1890	...	...	16th June.
Saturday, 26th July, 1890	...	...	14th July.

N. R. D. BOND,

Secretary.

491 (LATE 100) BOURKE STREET,

MELBOURNE.

Trained by T. Brown   **GRAND FLANEUR, 1880.**   Ridden by T. Hales
Hon W. A. Long

Trained by T. Lamond   **ZULU, 1881.**   Ridden by Gough
Mr C. McDonnell

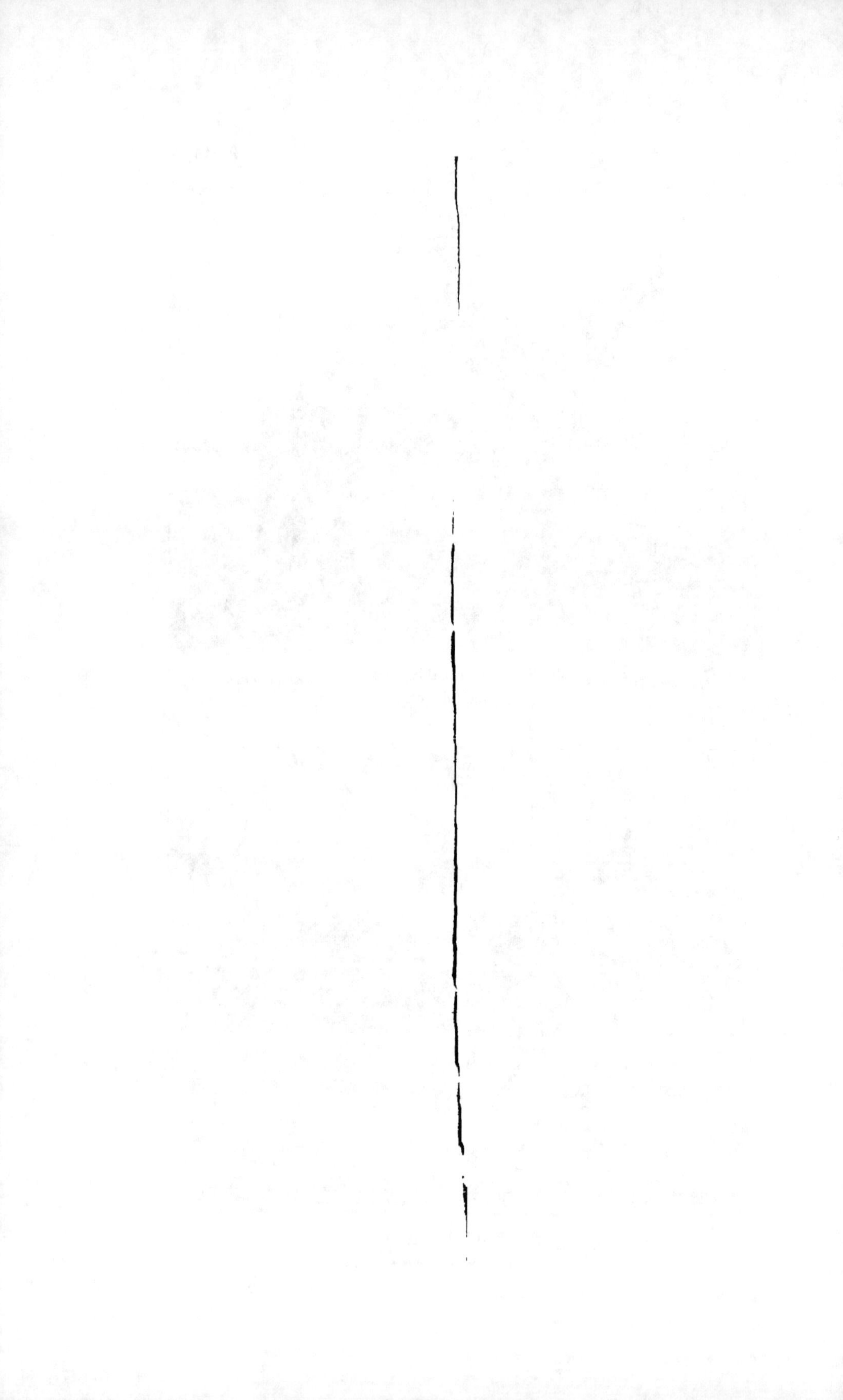

the latter lying on the outside. Totalisator passed Lothair at the corner, and led round the turn, and along the back. Approaching the bridge Napper Tandy took second place, whilst Riverton joined the leader, but was done with near the abattoirs; Napper Tandy also crying a go at the same time, leaving Progress slightly in advance of Lord Burleigh, Grand Flaneur, Lothair, Mata and Chester, who were in the order named, with Darriwell whipping in. Mata cut it before the turn into the straight, which was first entered by Lord Burleigh, who was slightly in advance of Progress and Lothair. ' Grand Flaneur, who was lying close on the inside, was at the distance post brought forward by Hales, and at once got on terms with the leaders. Lothair immediately dropped back and Progress led for a few yards, when Grand Flaneur came away, and won by a length, while Progress, after a splendid struggle with Lord Burleigh, beat him by half a head for second honors.

Time—3min 33¾secs.

Although only trained for the Derby of

1881,

in which he spreadeagled his field, there were many who considered Darebin would have the biggest say in the Cup race, and consequently he was made first favorite at 3 to 1. Away at the end of the betting was the cripple,

Zulu,

by Barbarian — Maiden's Blush, 50 to 1 being easily obtainable about him so little were his chances of winning considered. Darebin was brought to the post with the usual Dakin polish, and held a big reception, as did Waxy, who had numerous friends. The scarecrow appearance presented by Duchess excited general wonder that such an animal could ever have been made first favorite. First Water, Savanaka, and Santa Claus were all on the light side, but Odd Trick, who carried a lot of Ballarat money, was in excellent trim. Zulu and The Czar were both lame, and in fact considerable doubts were expressed about their being started. The betting was very heavy, and the

downfall of the favorites largely enriched the ring.

Value of stake, 1800 sovs. being a sweepstake of 20 sovs, with 500 added.

Mr. C. McDowall's blk c ZULU, Barbarian—Maiden's Blush, 4yrs, 5st 10lbs (Gough) 1
Mr. J. Morrison's br h THE CZAR by The Marquis — Dagmar, 5yrs, 6st 9lbs (Trahan) 2
Mr. T. Ivory's SWEETMEAT, by Yattendon—Sultana, 6yrs, 9st (Pigott) ... 3

Mr. C. G. Baldock's br h Wellington, 6yrs, 6st 11lbs (Yeomans) ; Mr. J. Croziers, junr.'s g h Savanaka, aged, 8st 7lbs (Colley) ; Mr. W. Pile's ch h First Water, 5yrs, 8st 7lbs (Wyman) ; Mr. H. Driver's b c Sir Modred, 4yrs, 8st 4lbs (Rawlings) ; Mr. R. Howie's g h Suwarrow, 5yrs 8st 3lbs (Dodd) ; Mr. T. Ivory's br h Lord Burleigh, 6yrs, 7st 11lbs (Francis) ; Mr. R. Wilson's ch h Odd Trick, 6yrs, 7st 9lbs (Walker) ; Mr. D. S. Wallace's ch c Waterloo, 4yrs, 7st 8lbs (O'Brien) ; Hon. J. White's br c Bathurst (Telphas) 4yrs, 7st 7lbs (Williamson) ; Mr. W. A. Long's blk g Trump Yoss, 6yrs, 7st 5lbs (Sullivan) ; Mr. M. Jacob's br c Canary, 4yrs, 7st 5lbs (Sullivan) ; Mr. A. K. Maitland's br h The Wandering Jew, 5yrs, 7st 11b (Burton) ; Mr. J. Whittingham's b c Chatterer, 4yrs, 7st (W. Murphy) ; Mr. P. Brennair's b c Creswick, 4yrs, 6st 13lbs (Gainsford); Mr. F. F. Watkins' br c Darebin, 3yrs, 6st 13lbs (Power) ; Captain Osborne's b c Wheatear, 3yrs, 6st 12lbs (Emsworth); Mr. R. J. Moore's b h Pawnbroker, 5yrs, 6st 10lbs (G. Williams); Mr. D. Melhado's b c Bandalbion, 4yrs, 6st 10lbs (Connors); Mr. H. Driver's b c Somnus, 3yrs, 6st 7lbs (Cracknell); Mr. G. Livingstone's br h Pollio, 5yrs, 6st 7lbs (Pears) ; Mr. E. De Mestre's b c Orient, 4yrs, 6st 6lbs (Riley) ; Mr. E. De Mestre's ch c Guinea, 4yrs, 6st 4lbs (Shean) ; Mr. R. Rowe's b h Waxy, 6yrs, 6st 11b (Nicholson) ; Mr. H. Herbert's b or br m Carmen, 4yrs, 5st 12lbs (Russell) ; Mr. H. Burnett's b or br f Coreena, 3yrs, 5st 10lbs (Ricketson) ; Mr. E. S. Jones' ch c Greyhound, 3yrs, 5st 9lbs (Kilby) ; Mr. D. Macpherson's br c Santa Claus 3yrs, 5st 9lbs (Bowes) ; Messrs. Skenes Bros. b f Duchess, 4ys, 5st 7lbs. (Young) ; Mr. F. Coker's blk c The Cockney, 3yrs, 5st 7lbs (Barr) ; Mr. R. Alexander's br m Oxalia, 5st 7lbs (Phillips).

Betting : 100 to 33 agst Darebin, 100 to 25 Waxy, 100 to 14 Odd Trick, 100 to 10 Duchess, 100 to 8 Wandering Jew and Santa Claus, 100 to 7 Sweetmeat, 100 to 5 Trump Yoss, The Czar, Waterloo, Creswick, Orient, Wellington, Savanaka, Pollio, Carmen, 100 to 4, Wheatear, Bathurst and Guinea, 100 to 2 Zulu.

Coreena caused some trouble at the start, bolting with her boy for fully half a mile, but at last the field of 33 was despatched to an excellent start, Oxalia, Wheatear and Somnus being first to move. Somnus was in front at the distance post, and led past the stand from Santa Claus, Bathurst, Waterloo and Darebin being next against the rails, and then came Suwarrow, Wandering Jew, Zulu, whose lameness seemed to disappear as the race proceeded, Carmen, Creswick, Odd Trick in a cluster, with the inevitable Lord Burleigh last. Santa Claus headed Somnus at the three-quarter mile post, and led along the back stretch with the favorite third. Then came Bathurst, Zulu, Trump Yoss, and half a dozen others, with Sweetmeat rapidly passing the stragglers. Zulu challenged Santa Claus near the abattoirs and took the lead, the order at the sheds being Zulu, Waxy, Darebin. At the half mile post a dog ran amongst the horses, and Wheatear threw Emsworth, who escaped with a severe shaking ; but a little further on Suwarrow was driven on the rails and broke the left leg of his jockey Dodd. Zulu had a clear lead of Waxy entering the straight, Trump Yoss, First Water and The Czar being close by, while Sweetmeat was coming up very fast. The Czar joined Waxy and Trump Yoss at the distance and drawing out immediately afterwards tried to reach Zulu, but failed, the cripple winning amidst intense excitement by three quarters of a length from The Czar, the same distance separating the latter from Sweetmeat, who finished third—a length behind Waxy.

Time—3min, 32¼ secs.

Amongst the long list of favorites for the Cup of

1882,

Sweet William was perhaps the one most feared by the books, as his name had been written scores of times in doubles with that of Navigator, who won the Derby. However they had no reason to grumble, as the victory of

The Assyrian,

by Countryman — Tinfinder, who started at 33 to 1, pulled them clean out of the mire. Mr. J. E. Savill had little or no hope of his winning until the rain came on, when he knew his chance had come, and he and his friends took several long shots just before starting. The St. Albans pair, Mistaken and Little Jack, next to Sweet William, were the favorites, then Odd Trick, Sylvanus and Darebin. Mistaken was thought to be favored by the rain, and hardened in price until he started at 5 to 1. When the Cup was run there was a perfect downfall, and after passing the stand onlookers could see little but a crowd of horses in front of which Stockwell's colors glittered through the driving rain, until coming home Assyrian was seen to be in front, much to the joy of the pencillers.

Value of stake, 2010 sovs., being a sweepstake of 20 sovs. each with 500 added.

Mr. J. E. Savill's br h THE ASSYRIAN, by Countryman —Tinfinder, 5yrs, 7st 13lbs (Hutchens) 1
Hon. T. Reiby's ch c STOCKWELL, by St. Albans—Edella, 4yrs, 7st 5lbs (Reilly) 2
Mr. E. De Mestre's br c GUDARZ, by Yattendon—Luna, 4yrs, 7st 7lbs (Gainsford) 3

Mr. F. F. Dakins' br c Darebin, 4yrs, 9st 9lbs (Power); Mr. T. Ivory's br h Lord Burleigh, aged, 8st 12lbs (Pigott); Mr. J. Crozier, jr s g h Savanaka, aged, 8st 9lbs (Yeomans); Mr. J. Crozier, jr's ch h First Water, 6yrs, 8st 6lbs (Colley); Mr. W. R. Hall's br c Cunnamulla, 4yrs, 8st 2lbs (M‘Grade); Mr. T. Wentworth's br c The Drummer, 4yrs, 8st 1lbs (Williamson) ; Mr. E. Week's b h Pollio, 6yrs, 7st 13lbs (Kilby); Hon. J. White's b or b c Segenhoe, 3yrs, 7st 12lbs (Murphy) ; Mr. C. Wilson's ch h Odd Trick, aged, 7st 12lbs (Burton) ; Mr. E. De Mestre s b c Sweet William, 4yrs, 7st 11lbs (Hales) ; Mr. H. James' b c Santa Claus, 4yrs, 7st 7lbs (Trahan) ; Captain Rossi's b h Lord Lisgar, 5yrs, 7st 7lbs (Thomas) : Mr. P. J. M‘Alister's b f Jessie, 3yrs, 7st 6lbs (Davis) ; Mr. E. Weeks' b c Sylvanus, 3yrs, 6st 13lbs (Rayner) ; Mr. W. Branch's b c Little Jack, 3yrs, 6st 8lbs (Moore) ; Mr. S. G. Cook's b c Anglesey, 3yrs, 6st 4lbs (Boase) ; Mr. T. M. Jordan's br c Standard Bearer, 3yrs 6st 4lbs (Quinn) : Mr. W. H. Gray's b c Flying Jib, 4yrs 6st 6lbs (Barr); Mr. W. Branch's b c Mistaken, 3yrs, 6st 6lbs Mr. J. A. Lang's ch c King of the Vale, 3yrs, 6st 4lbs (Cracknell) ; Mr. B. M. Osborne s b f Brunette, 3yrs, 6st 2lbs (Ellis). Mr. E. Week's c h Sting, 3 yrs, 7st 5lbs (O'Brien.)

Betting 4 to 1 agst Sweet William, 5 to 1 Mistaken, 8 to 1 Little Jack, 12 to 1 Odd Trick, 15 to 1 Stockwell, 20 to 1 Darebin, Sting, Cunnamulla, Savanaka, Sylvanus, King of the Vale, 25 to 1 Pollio, 33 to 1 The Assyrian, Jessie, Gudarz, The Drummer, 100 to 1 Segenhoe.

Cunnamulla as usual played up at the start, and lashing out struck the favorite on the thigh, thereby materially interfering with his chances. An excellent start was at last effected, Jessie and Gudarz obtaining a slight lead from Flying Jib, Stockwell, Mistaken and Santa Claus Mistaken was in front for a few strides at the tan, but gave place to Flying Jib, who took his field

BARTLETT'S
RAILWAY HOTEL,
ELIZABETH STREET,
CORNER OF FLINDERS LANE.

A. H. BARTLETT

BEGS to refer his former Patrons and the Public generally to the extensive transformation of the Old House to its present most elegant, fashionable and comfortable appearance—refurnished and redecorated in the chaste Oriental style.

The professional and experienced Cook still presides over the Culinary Department with additional aid.

The New Bar, with its elaborate fittings, is well worth a visit from Old Friends from the Country.

None but the Best Brands will be available in any and all Liquors.

This Hotel is situate in close proximity to the Flinders Street, and within five minutes of the Spencer Street Railway Station.

Trams Pass the Door.   Every Convenience for Visitors.

HOT AND COLD BATHS ON EACH FLAT!

NIGHT PORTERS.

A. H BARTLETT   -   -   *Proprietor.*

CALDWELL'S
Australian Wine Company, Ltd.

PURE   OLD
WINES  WINES

SPECIALITIES :

Claret.   Chablis.
Ngarveno Hock.

N.B.—Ask for **Caldwell's**, and see that the Company's name is on each bottle.

Registered Office, 495 Collins Street.

THE ASSYRIAN, 1882.
Mr J. E. Savill

Trained by owner   Ridden by C. Hutchens

MARTINI—HENRI, 1883.
Hon. J. White

Trained by M. Fennelly   Ridden by J. Williamson

past the stand at a merry pace. Rounding the turn Stockwell was in front, his immediate attendants being Gudarz and Mistaken. Then came in good positions Segenhoe, Flying Jib, Assyrian, Santa Claus, and Little Jack, with Lord Burleigh last. Stockwell still in the lead forced the pace along the back to the bridge, where Flying Jib was done with, and Mistake fell back. The Assyrian and Darebin chased Stockwell and Gudarz into the straight, with Sweet William and Segenhoe next, all the rest being beaten. The Assyrian on the outside and Darebin on the inside, were with Stockwell at the distance, and despite the splendid efforts made by the topweight who had made such a gallant run, The Assyrian won by a length after heading Stockwell at the carriage paddock. Half a length behind Stockwell came Gudarz, who had beaten Darebin in the last few yards for third honors.

Time—3min. 40secs.

Previous Cup meetings have been notable for the overthrow of favorites, but that of

1883

was an exception in this way. Early in the season First Water had been backed to win nearly £80,000. Claptrap, Commotion, Archie and half a dozen others also carried heaps of money. But for once the public were right in installing

Martini Henri,

by Musket — Sylvia, first favourite, as his sire and dam justified their verdict by winning easily, while Commotion struggled into third place, and the cheers for the victory of the favorite, were quite equalled by those for the gallant run into a place, by a horse that always held the affections of the public.

Value of stake, 2657 sovs., being a sweepstakes of 20 sovs. each, with 1000 sovs. added.

Hon. J. White's b c MARTINI HENRI, by Musket—Sylvia, 3yrs, 7st 5lbs (Williamson)   1
Mr. T. Barnfield's ch c FIRST WATER, by Fireworks—The Gem, aged, 8st (McGrade)   2
Hon. W. Pearson's b h COMMOTION, by Panic—Evening Star, 5yrs, 10st 1lb (Trahan)   3

Mr. W. Gannon's br h Sweet William. 5yrs, 9st 5lbs (Yeomans) ; Mr. W. Bailey's ch h Stockwell, 5yrs, 8st 13lbs (Gaghan) ; Mr. J. Mayo's b h The Gem, 5yrs 9st 4lbs (Huxley) ; Mr. W. Hall's br h Cunnamulla, 5yrs, 8st 13lbs (Colley) ; Mr. A. F. Smart's br c Archie, 3yrs, 8st 3lbs (Gough) ; Mr. D. S. Wallace's br c Calma, 4yrs, 8st 7lbs (M. O'Brien) ; Hon. W. Pearson's b c Magnet. 4yrs, 8st (Power) ; Mr. E. De Mestre's br c Nicholas, 4yrs 8st (Hales) : Mr. S. Weeks' b h Pollio, aged, 7st 12lbs (Burton) ; Mr. S. Barnard's ch c Dirk Hatterick, 3yrs, 7st 10lbs (Boase) ; Mr. S. G. Cook's b c Anglesey, 4yrs, 7st 10lbs (Robertson) ; Mr. J. Stewart's b c Kingsdale, 3yrs, 7st 8lbs (Strickland) ; Mr. H. James' b h Santa Claus, 5yrs, 7st 5lbs (Walker) ; Mr. H. Bowler's b c Aide-de-Camp. 4yrs, 7st 4lbs (Gainsford) ; Mr. J. Whittingham's b or br c Claptrap. 4yrs, 7st 3lbs (Cracknell) ; Mr. T. Sampson's b h Recovery, 5yrs, 7st 2lbs (Kelso) ; Mr. W. Branch's br c Dukedom, 3yrs, 7st (Moore) ; Mr. C. H. T. Hart's br h Kohinoor 5yrs, 7st (Thornton) ; Hon. J. White's gr c Despot, 4yrs, 7st (Ellis) ; Mr. S. Mahon's br f Lesbia, 4yrs, 6st 12lbs (English) ; Mr. J. H. Aldridge's br c Sardius, 3yrs, 6st 11lbs (C. Hutchins) ; Mr. J. Wilson's ns br m Linda, 5yrs, 6st 10lbs (Fallon) ; Mr. J. McKenzie's b m Kathleen Mavourneen, 6yrs, 6st 9lbs (Barr) ; Mr. W. Gordon's ch f Bis Bis, 3yrs, 6st 8lbs (F. Hutchins)' Mr. D. S. Wallace's b c Le Grand, 3yrs, 7st 5lbs (Nerriker) ; Mr. J. Monday's br c First Demon, 3yrs, 6st 12lbs (Nicholson).

Betting : 5 to 1 agst Martini Henri, 6 to 1 Despot, 7 to 1 Claptrap, 10 to 1 First Demon, Calma. 12 to 1 Aide-de-Camp, 14 to 1 Sardius, Nicholas, 16 to 1 Dirk Hatterick, 20 to 1 Commotion, 25 to 1 Le Grand, First Water. 33 to 1 Sweet William, Stockwell, Archie and Pollio. 50 to 100 to 1 others.

Mr. Watson was fairly successful with his field of 29, and got them away to a good start. Claptrap led Archie and Dukedom across the tan and past the stand, where the order was Claptrap, Archie, Despot, Dukedom, Martini Henri, Linda, First Demon, Aide-de-Camp, and the rest in a bunch. Despot slipped when rounding the turn and nearly fell, thus interfering seriously with Calma. Linda was in front along the river side, being followed by Archie and Claptrap, Dukedom and Martini Henri. Aide-de-Camp came next, lying in a good position. Archie and Linda changed places at the bridge, the order of the others being Claptrap, Dukedom, First Demon, and Martini Henri, First Water, and Commotion, the latter being lengths in front of the ruck, whilst the leaders were close together. The pace now began to tell, Archie being the first to tire, then Linda gave way. Till half a mile from home Claptrap was in front, with Commotion, First Water, Aide-de-Camp, Calma, Martini Henri following closely in the order named. Commotion ran up to Claptrap at the home turn, and came into the straight in front of the whilom leader and First Water, First Demon and Sardius, the latter having made a fast run from the rear division. Then followed Martini Henri and Dukedom. Claptrap and Dukedom gave way at the bottom of the paddock, leaving Commotion in advance, only to be headed when half way home by Martini Henri and First Water, the former gaining a clear lead, which he maintained, Williamson landing him an easy winner by a length and a half from First Water who, after a hard fight, beat Commotion for second place by a neck, the latter only gaining his gamely won third honor by a head from First Demon, after whom came Sardius.

Time—3min. 30½secs.

Fully a score of horses were at one time or another installed as favorites in

1884.

The public pet, Commotion, was deservedly backed, his consistent running into prominent positions under crushing weights showing that he was well worthy of support. Of these various favorites, Off Color perhaps held the pride of place, but at last the public settled down on

Malua,

by St. Albans—Edella, who, when the hour of trial came, did not belie his friends' expectations. As showing the estimation in which Commotion was held by the public, he was backed one day to win £10,000, most of the wagers to make up this amount being comparatively small. The downfall of Bargo, the Derby favorite, and who had been backed heavily to win the Cup, made the books look joyous, whilst about Hastings and Plunger, of whom great things were expected, and Blink Bonny, there was sufficient danger to make an unsettled market. Of the twenty-four horses that weighed out Hastings and Malua were the two favorites at 6 to 1 at starting, and were fairly mobbed in the paddock.

Value of stakes, 2477 sovs., being a sweepstakes of 20 sovs. each, with 1000 added.

Mr. J. Inglis's br h MALUA, by St. Albans—Edella, 5yrs, 9st 9lbs (A. Robertson) 1
Hon. W. Pearson's br h COMMOTION, by Panic—Evening Star, 6yrs, 9st 12lbs (Power) 2
Hon. W. Pearson's b g PLAUSIBLE, by Vagabond—Plaudit, 5yrs, 6st 12lbs (Murphy) 3

Mr. J. Redfearn's br h The Plunger, 5yrs, 8st 11lbs (Pigott) ; Mr. W. Branch's Off Color, 4yrs, 8st 10lbs (Moore) ; Mr. J. Mondy's br c Bristol, 4yrs, 8st 1lb (Colley) ; Mr. T. Sampson's b h Hastings, 5yrs, 7st 13lbs (McGrade) ; Mr. S. Miller's Boolka, 5yrs, 7st 7lbs (Olds) ; Mr. R. G. Talbot's c m Blink Bonny, 6yrs, 7st 7lbs (Williamson) ; Hon. G. White's b c Bargo, 3yrs, 7st 6lbs (Hales) ; Mr. J. A. Lang's br c Vergy, 4yrs, 7st 6lbs (O'Brien) : Mr. W. J. Forrester's br g Bonnie Bee, aged, 7st 5lbs (Trahan) ; Mr. W. J. Whittingham's br h Claptrap, 5rs, 7st 4lbs (Ivemy) ; Mr. W. F. Smart's ch f Brown and Rose, 3yrs, 7st 3lbs (Gough) ; Mr. M. Jacob's ch c Hill Top, 5yrs, 7st 2lbs (Nicholson) ; Mr. A. R. Robertson's ch c The Broker, 7st 1lb (Ellridge) ; Mr. E. P. Wilson's br or blk c Signor, 4yrs, 6st 3lbs (G. Williams) ; Mr. S. Key's b h Lord Clifden, aged, 6st 12lbs (R. Davis) ; Mr. E. W. Ellis's ch c Lord Wilton, 4yrs, 6st 11lbs (Sanders) ; M. W. A. Gray's br c Hippogriff, 3yrs, 6st 11lbs (Cracknell) ; Mr. M. Griffin's ch h Battalious, 5yrs, 6st 13lbs (Kelso) ; Mr. W. M. Robertson's b c Anchorite, 4yrs, 6st 9lbs (T. Williams) ; Hon. J. White's br c Tremando, 3yrs, 6st 9lbs (Ellis) ; Mr. J. Whittingham's ch c Merrimu, 3yrs, 6st 8lbs (Bacchus).

Betting : 6 to 1 each Malua and Hastings, 12 to 1 The Plunger, Plausible, Blink Bonny, Vergy, 14 to 1 Hill Top and Bargo, 15 to 1 Off Color, 20 to 1 Commotion, Claptrap, Anchorite.

An excellent start was obtained, of which, however, Plausible did not take full advantage, and with Claptrap, was left to follow the others across the tan. Passing the stand Signor led Bargo, Anchorite, and Tremando at a great speed, the order of those following immediately being Boolka, Commotion, Malua, Battalious, Off Color and Vergy, all however close together, whilst Claptrap was last. Signor led his horses round the turn, The Broker having, however, run up third, whilst the next places were occupied by Lord Wilton, Anchorite and Plunger. Along the river side and past the bridge, the pace was very hot, Signor being still in front, till near the abattoirs, where Plunger joined and passed him at the sheds. Plausible, Malua, and Commotion now ran into forward places, The

CAMPBELL & SONS,

AUCTIONEERS,

Horse, Cattle & Property Salesmen

KIRK'S BAZAAR,

Bourke Street, Melbourne.

VICTORIA HORSE BAZAAR.

Robertson, Capes & Co., Stock & Station Agents.

Daily Sales of Horses, Vehicles, &c.

Victoria Horse Bazaar, Bourke Street, Melbourne.

Monthly Sales of Cattle, Horses, &c.

Lancefield : First Monday of Month.   Gisborne : On Last Saturday of Month.

BRANCH OFFICE: CHAUNCY STREET, LANCEFIELD.

G. W. CRABBE & CO.,

Bill Brokers and Financial Agents,

6B IMPERIAL CHAMBERS, BANK PLACE

(Established 1864),

Have large SUMS to LEND on City and Suburban Properties, at 5½, 6. and 7 per cent. Principals only dealt with. Bills Discounted daily from 10 per cent. Public companies underwritten or floated on commission.

Agents in London and Liverpool for English business.

WITT'S ROSE COLLYRIUM

OR EYE LOTION.

Strengthens the Eyes, Cures Inflammations, Blight and Sore Eyes when other eye lotions and medical treatment have failed, as proved by numerous testimonials. The originals may be seen at the establishment of the proprietors, where also local and other references to cures effected may be obtained.

1s. 3d. and 2s. per Bottle.

Prepared only by the Proprietors, WITT & CO., Chemists Prahran Melbourne and sold by Chemists and Vendors of Patent Medicines

Wholesale—Felton and Co., Duerdin and Sainsbury, Rocke, Tompsitt and Co., Melbourne ; Elliott Bros., Sydney.

Trained by I. Foulsham   **MALUA, 1884.**   Ridden by Alec. Robertson
M? J.O. Inglis

Trained by T. Wilson   **SHEET ANCHOR, 1885.**   Ridden by Mick O'Brien
M? M.Loughlin

Broker and Lord Wilton being completely done with, whilst Hastings had come forward and was close to the leading division. The Plunger led into the straight from Plausible, who headed him shortly afterwards, only to be cut down in his turn by Commotion, who was loudly proclaimed the winner. Malua, however, who had been lying fourth, shot out and, catching Commotion when half way home, won by three quarters of a length; Commotion second, two lengths from Plausible, who was third.

Time—3min. 31¾secs.

A noteworthy feature of the following year was that no less than 35 horses faced the starter in

1885,

this being the largest field ever started in a Melbourne Cup. Favorites were plentiful, Nordenfeldt, Despot, Trenton, Grace Darling, and half a dozen others having their turn in the market, while not a few pinned their faith to

Sheet Anchor,

by St. Albans—Queen Mary, who did not disappoint his friends.

As usual, the attendance far exceeded the hundred thousand limit, while the weather was excellent. In the paddock Nordenfeldt, Despot and Grace Darling claimed most attention, although the Ballarat men crowded round Sheet Anchor, and much admiration was lavished on Trenton.

Value of stakes, 2912 sovs., being a handicap sweepstakes of 20 sovs. each, with 1000 sovs. added.

Mr M. Loughlin's br h SHEET ANCHOR, by St. Albans - Queen Mary, aged, 7st 11lbs (M. O'Brien) 1
Mr. J. G. Reid's ch m GRACE DARLING, by The Diver—Zoe, 6yrs, 7st 12lbs (J. Williams) 2
Mr. D. O'Brien's ch m TRENTON, by Musket — Frailty, 4yrs, 9st 13lbs (Robertson) 3

Mr. R. G. Talbot's ch m Blink Bonny, aged, 8st 5lbs (Blair); Mr. A. Halinbourg's br c Acolyte, 4yrs, 8st 11b (Sanders); Mr. S. W. Ellis's ch h Lord Wilton, 5yrs, 8st (Ivemy); Mr. C. J. Brackenreg's br h Tom Brown, 5yrs, 8st (Gainsford); Mr. Phillips' b h Kit Nubbles, 6yrs, 7st 12lbs (Colley); Mr. J. D. Robertson's br h Coriolanus, aged, 7st 12lbs (Moore); Mr. M. Bryant's br h Bosworth, aged, 7st 9lbs (Riley); Mr. A. F. Smart's b h Warwick, 6yrs, 7st 9lbs (J. Gough); Mr. A. Halinbourg's b h St. Lawrence, 6yrs, 7st 9lbs (Smith); Hon. W. Pearson's b g Plausible, 6yrs, 7st 8lbs (Power); Hon. W. Robinson's ch c Liverpool, 4yrs 7st 8lbs (Derritt); Mr. J. Whittingham's br h Prometheus, 6yrs, 7st 6lbs (Trahan); Mr. A. R. Robertson's b or br c Dunlop, 3yrs, 7st 6lbs (Foon); Hon. W. Robinson's b or br c Thunderbolt, 3yrs, 7st 5lbs (Huxtable); Mr. T. Henty's b c Stornoway, 4yrs, 7st 5lbs (Musgrove); Hon. J. White's br c Nordenfeldt, 3yrs, 7st 5lbs (Ellis); Mr. W. Condron's br h Velocipede, 5yrs, 7st 4lbs (Burton); Mr. M. Jacobs' blk h Hill Top, 6yrs, 7st 4lbs (Darke); Mr. C. H. T. Hart's br h St. John, 5yrs, 7st 3lbs (Flanagan); Hon. J. White's g h Despot, 6yrs, 7st 2lbs (M'Auliffe); Mr. W. Hall's ch c Lord Exeter, 4yrs, 8st 11lbs (Williamson); Mr. A. F. Smart's ch f Brown and Rose, 4yrs, 7st (A. Gough); Mr. R. Rouse, junr. s ch h Wing, 5yrs, 7st 5lbs (Nerriker); Mr. M. Loughlin's b g Britisher aged, 6st 11lbs (Fallon); Mr. W. Kelso's br c First Chester, 3yrs, 6st 10lbs (G. Williams); Hon. W. Pearson's b c Arsenal, 3yrs, 6st 9lbs (Brown); Mr. H J. Bowler's b m Minerva, 5yrs, 6st 8lbs (Curran); Mr. M. Jacobs' b c Metal, 4yrs, 6st 6lbs (Redfearn); Mr. F. Henty's b c Cyclops, 3yrs, 6st 3lbs (Johnson); Mr. A. F. Bradshaw's ch h Yellow Hammer, 5yrs, 6st 5lbs (Guy); Mr. H. L. Oxenham's b f Cerise and Blue, 4yrs, 6st (Gorry); Mr. S. Davis's br m Lesbia, 6yrs, 6st 5lbs (M'Donald).

Betting: 5 to 1 agst Nordenfeldt, 6 to 1 Trenton 8 to 1 Despot, 10 to 1 Liverpool, 14 to 1 Sheet Anchor and Stornoway, 15 to 1 Kit Nubbles, 20 to 1 Acolyte, Grace Darling, Warwick, Brown and Rose, Cerise and Blue. 25 to 100 to 1 others.

Prometheus was first away, with First Chester, Thunderbolt, Nordenfeldt, St. John and Lord Exeter in a cluster close behind, and in this order they thundered past the stand, Grace Darling being noticeable behind the main body, while Yellow Hammer, the latter day Lord Burleigh, whipped in. First Chester and Thunderbolt closed on Prometheus rounding the turn, the former taking the lead and maintaining it along the river side, Prometheus, Nordenfeldt, St. John and Velocipede being a length or so away. Velocipede got on even terms with First Chester at the mile post, whilst immediately behind came Sheet Anchor and Nordenfeldt, together, with Liverpool on the outside and Grace Darling in the middle of the ruck, apparently blocked. Velocipede remained at the head of affairs right round to the home turn, where the order was Velocipede, Sheet Anchor, Lesbia, Brown and Rose and Nordenfeldt, who were close together. Inside the straight Sheet Anchor made a rush forward, Velocipede falling back, and Nordenfeldt taking second place. Grace Darling, who had twice been disappointed, now threaded her horses, and coming home with a very exciting rush headed Nordenfeldt, but failed to reach Sheet Anchor, who won by a head, Trenton struggling into third place a neck in advance of Nordenfeldt.

Time—3min. 29½secs.

The transactions in the betting market were especially lively in the following year, and many of the ringmen had good cause to remember the Cup of

1886,

since although an outsider won, he had been heavily backed in Sydney, and even at the last moment in Melbourne. The public, however, had so persistently put their coin on Trident, Ben Bolt, Trenton, Silvermine and others, that the books had plenty of public money with which to pay the losses on

Arsenal,

by Goldsbrough—Powder.

Considerably over 100,000 people attended, whilst the efforts made by the committee of the V.R.C. to provide for their patrons both on the stand and on the hill were much appreciated. In the saddling paddock Trident was the hero of the hour, and his training and aristocratic appearance gave his friends great hopes. Ben Bolt had many admirers, especially amongst the clever division that had profited so largely by his win at Caulfield.

Value of stake, 3465 sovs., being a sweepstake of 20 sovs. each, with 2000 added.

Mr. W. Gannon's br c ARSENAL, by Goldsbrough — Powder, 4yrs, 7st 4lbs (carried 7st 5lbs (English) ... 1

Mr. W. Cooper's b h TRENTON, by Musket - Frailty, 5yrs, 9st 5lbs (Robertson) 2

Mr. H. R. Falkiner's blk or g h SILVERMINE, by Napoleon — Silverhair, 5yrs, 7st 13lbs (McGrade) 3

Mr. J. O. Inglis's b h Malua, aged, 10st (Owner) ; Hon. W. Pearson's b h Commotion, aged, 9st 9lbs (Power) ; Mr. M. Loughlin's br h Sheet Anchor, aged, 9st (Colley) ; Mr. J. G. Reid's ch m Grace Darling, aged, 8st 11lbs (J. Williams) ; Mr. W. Locke's br c Isonomy, 4yrs, 8st 3lbs (Quinn) ; Hon. J. White's g c Monte Christo, 4yrs, 8st (Ellis) ; Mr. T. Jones's br h Bohemian, 8st (Gallagher) ; Mr. M. Loughlin's b g Britisher, aged, 7st 13lbs (Fallon) ; Mr. R. K. Maitland's b h Meteor, 6yrs, 9st 11lbs (Fiddes) ; Mr. S. Miller's br h Boolka, aged, 7st 10lbs (Olds) ;

Mr. W. Strickland's b h Ben Bolt, 5yrs, 7st 10lbs (O'Brien) ; Mr. T. Coffey's br c Kitawa, 4yrs, 7st 9lbs (Cox) ; Mr. J. R. Smith's b g Lancer, 6yrs, 7st 8lbs (B. Williams) ; Mr. F. Henty's b c Cyclops, 4yrs, 7st 7lbs (Williamson) ; Hon. J. White's ch c Trident, 3yrs, 7st 7lbs (Hales) ; Mr. M. Jacobs' b h Metal, 5yrs, 8st 2lbs (Sanders) ; Hon. W. A. Long's br f Crossfire, 3yrs, 7st 1lb (J. Bence) ; Mr. R. Orr's b c Recall, 4yrs, 6st 11lbs (Gorry) ; Hon J. Eales' br g Myall King, 4yrs, 6st 9lbs (Casey) ; Mr. W. Duggen's n ch c Lord William, 3yrs, 6st 9lbs (Gough) ; Mr. W. Moran's br h Little John, 6yrs, 6st 7lbs (Cracknell) ; Mr. W. E. Boyd's b c Bravo, 3yrs, 6st 6lbs (Campbell) ; Hon. J. White's ch c Hexham, 4yrs, 6st 5lbs (Huxley) ; Mr. R. G. Talbot's b c Highland Chief, 4yrs, 6st (Morrison) : Mr. J. Calvert's blk g Jack Roach, 5yrs, 6st (D. Williams).

Betting: 9 to 2 agst Trident, 6 to 1 Ben Bolt and Isonomy, 8 to 1 Meteor, 10 to 1 Little John, 12 to 1 Trenton and Malua, 15 to Silvermine, 20 to 1 Arsenal, Commotion, and Britisher. 25 to 50 to 1 others.

An excellent start was obtained, although Little John and Grace Darling got away badly. Trenton, who was against the rails, was the first to move, but crossing the tan, Silvermine and Recall were in front together, whilst behind them came Bravo, Meteor, Hexham, Jack Roach, and Trenton in line. Silvermine led past the stand a length from Bravo, and then came Metal, Arsenal, Isonomy, Meteor, Jack Roach, Recall and Hexham closely. Rounding the turn Boolka was close to the leaders, Silvermine still leading his field until, at the bridge, Hexham took command. Little John was a score of lengths behind his horses, and Grace Darling hopelessly following him. Hexham led Arsenal by half a length at the abattoirs, Silvermine being two lengths behind. Then came the favorite, Lord William, Ben Bolt, Trenton, and Bohemian in a bunch. Arsenal and Hexham were together at the sheds, Hexham having the inside running, whilst Trident was only a length away, with Silvermine, Crossfire, Lord William and Trenton close up. Hexham fell back at the turn into the straight, and Arsenal coming forward was never caught, although Silvermine made a futile effort to get on even terms with him, but at the half distance had himself to succumb to Trenton who, after a brilliant attempt to reach Arsenal, finished half a length behind him, and a length in front of Silvermine.

Time—3min. 31secs.

Trained by H. Rayner   **ARSENAL, 1886**   Ridden by English
Mr. W. Gannon

Trained by J. Nicholson   **DUNLOP 1887**   Ridden by T. Sanders
Mr. R. Donovan

The wholesale manner in which cash betting had been taken up of late years, and the abolition of the big sweeps, comparatively little was done in the market on the Cup of

1887

except in big lines until shortly before the eventful day. Australian Peer, Oakleigh, Recall, Silvermine and several others were in succession top of the list, but at last the pride of place was given to Meteor. In the meantime a few knowing ones were taking all the longshots they could manage about

Dunlop,

by Neckersgat—Etta, whose owner and trainer were very sanguine as to his chances. The correctness of their judgment was shown by the only horse they feared, Silvermine, finishing second. The crowd was great, if not greater than usual.

Value of stakes, 4885 sovs., being a sweepstakes of 20 sovs. each, with 2500 sovs. and a trophy value 100 sovs. added.

Mr. R. Donovan's b or br h DUNLOP by Neckersgat — Etta, 5yrs, 8st 3lbs (Sanders) 1

Mr. W. Cooper's blk or gr h SILVER-MINE, by Napoleon — Silverhair, 6yrs, 8st 3lbs (Robertson) 2

Mr. W. Gannon's b or br c THE AUSTRALIAN PEER, Darebin—Stockdove, 3yrs, 7st 5lbs (Gorry) 3

Mr. S. Nathan's b h Sardius, aged, 8st 5lbs (Burton); Hon. W. Robinson's b h Thunderbolt, 5yrs, 7st 8lbs (Gallagher); Hon. J. White's ch c Abercorn, 3yrs, 7st 7lbs (Hales); Mr. R. Orr's b h Recall, 5yrs, 7st 5lbs (Power); Mr. M. Loughlin's b h Oakleigh, 5yrs, 7st 4lbs (Fielder); Hon. W. Robinson's ch c Silver Prince, 4yrs, 7st 3lbs (Cochrane); Mr. W. C. Cooper's b c Niagara, 3yrs, 7st 3lbs (Trahan); Mr. R. K. Maitland's b h Meteor, aged 7st 2lbs (Fiddes); Hon. J. White's ch c Cranbourne, 3yrs, 6st 12lbs (O'Keefe); Mr G. Osborne's b h Algerian, 5yrs, 6st 12lbs (Nerriker); Mr. S. G. Cook's ch c Remus, 5yrs, 6st 11lbs (Cracknell); Mr. A. Harvey's ch c Pakeha, 3yrs, 6st 6lbs (O'Conner); Mr. E. Mitchelson's b c Tranter, 3yrs, 6st 5lbs (Walker); Mr. S. G. Cook's ch f The Charmer, 3yrs, 6st 10lbs (O'Neill); Mr. J. Cohen's br c Jebusite, 3yrs, 6st 3lbs (Howie).

Betting—5 to 1 Meteor, 6 to 1 The Australian Peer and Algerian, 7 to 1 Oakleigh, 14 to 1 each Silvermine and Recall, 15 to 1 each Remus and Silver Prince, 20 to 1 Dunlop, Niagara, Cranbrook, Trenton, 25 to 40 to 1 others.

Mr. Watson got his field of 18 away to an excellent start, Pakeha, Silver Prince and Dunlop moving off first, only to be passed by Algerian, who led until entering the course proper, where Silver Prince shot out and was in front past the stand from Tranter, Thunderbolt and The Charmer. Then came Oakleigh and Remus, whilst Sardius was last, a position he doggedly maintained throughout the race. Silver Prince still led round the turn, The Charmer's nose being at his girth, whilst just behind came Algerian, then Tranter, Remus, Thunderbolt and Pakeha, with Australian Peer and Recall close up. This order was maintained along the river side, Silvermine and Meteor whipping in the main body. Passing the bridge Algerian was second to Silver Prince, whilst Australian Peer, Cranbrook, Meteor and Silvermine had forged forward into good positions. Algerian and Silver Prince led alternately past the abattoirs and round the turn, their immediate attendants being Cranbrook and Remus, but when nearing the sheds, Dunlop ran up to Silver Prince who fell back. Algerian led into the straight from Cranbrook, Dunlop, Silvermine, Australian Peer and Recall. Immediately after entering the straight Dunlop came forward and won after an excellent race by a long length from Silvermine in the shortest time on record. Two lengths behind came Australian Peer.

Time—3min. 28½secs.

The public do not seem to have been quite alive to Dunlop's merits, though "Asmodeus" and "Augur" both drew attention to the wonderful improvement noticeable in his condition during the last month, and his running in the Caulfield Cup should certainly have recommended him to stronger support. He certainly proved himself one of the best and fastest horses which have contested for the great race; and the determined and scientific manner in which Saunders piloted him to victory in the fastest time—3min. 28½secs. on record—showed that the stable was justified in putting their money on, which they did to such an extent as to secure a nice little pile for owner and rider, as well as that portion of the public who had received the "tip," and some nice little pickings were made by those in the secret. This brings us to

1888

early in the season of which year large sums were invested on Spade Guinea, Cyclops, Dick Swiveller, The Yeoman, Bravo, Australian Peer, Arsenal and others. All through, however, a quiet division kept putting up their dollars on

Mentor,

and after a while the public followed suit. A sensational gallop by Whakawai sent him forward in the betting until the strong support given by the Caulfield crowd to Chicago made him favourite.

Being Exhibition year, there were many more strangers present than in previous years, 1880 not excepted. Chicago attracted much attention, whilst Mentor, the sensational Whakawai, Carlyon, Australian Peer and Darebin had many friends who watched their toilets anxiously.

Value of stake £4885, being a sweepstake of 25sovs. each with 3000sovs. and a trophy value 150sovs. added.

Mr. D. S. Wallace's b c MENTOR, by Swiveller—Nightmare, 4yrs, 8st 3lbs (O'Brien)   1
Mr. S. L. West's b c TRADITION, by Richmond—Bridal Wreath, 4yrs, 6st 11lbs (Aspinall)   2
Mr. S. G. Cook's ch g THE YEOMAN, by The Englishman — Springtime, 5yrs, 7st 8lbs (Rammage)   3

Mr. W. Gannon's b or br c The Australian Peer, 3yrs, 9st 8lbs (Power) ; Mr. J. O. Inglis's b h Malua, aged, 9st 7lbs (Owner) ; Hon. J. White's br c Carlyon, 4yrs, 9st 3lbs (Hales) ; Mr. W. Gannon's br h Arsenal, 6yrs, 9st (Ivemy) ; Mr. H. Strickland's b h Ben Bolt, aged, 8st 9lbs (Ettridge) ; Mr. W. T. Jones' b h Bravo, 5yrs, 8st 5lbs (Boase) ; Mr. S. G. Cook's b h Cyclops, 6yrs, 8st 3lbs (Dalton) ; Mr. R. Orr's b h Recall, 6yrs, 8st 3lbs (Sanders) ; Mr. H. Haines' ch m Spade Guinea, 6yrs, 8st 1lb (Harris) ; Mr. T. Sampson's g g Aristocrat, 5yrs, 8st (F. Smith) ; Messrs. Husband and Nicholl's b c Dick Swiveller, 4yrs, 7st 10lbs (A. Smith) ; Mr. M. O'Shanassy's br h Chicago, 5yrs, 7st 9lbs (Campbell) ; Hon. E. Mitchelson's bl c Whakawai, 4yrs, 7st 7lbs (T. Brown) ; Mr. M. Welch ns ch c Lord Headington, 4yrs, 7st 5lbs (Tomlin) ; Mr. W. Gannon's br c Melos, 3yrs, 7st 5lbs (Dunhey) ; Hon. J. White's br g Ensign, 3yrs 7st 5lbs (Huxley) ;

Mr. H. Oxenham's ch h Phaon, 6yrs, 7st 3lbs (Delaney) ; Mr. W. Gannon's b or br c Touchstone, 4yrs, 7st 3lbs (Fielder) ; Mr. C. Collins' ch h Newmaster, 5yrs, 7st 2lbs (Hayes) ; Mr. T. Sampson's b f Maggie, 3yrs, 7st (Archer) ; Mr. J. Murray's br h King of the West, 6yrs, 6st 11lbs (Coad) ; Mr. J. Barnard's b h E.D., 6yrs, 6st 8lbs (Ring) ; Sir W. J. Clarke's br h Menotti, 5yrs, 6st 7lbs (Morrison) ; Mr. G. T. Chirnside's blk f Beryl, 3yrs, 6st 7lbs (Bloomfield) ; Mr. S. Miller's b f Ilex, 3yrs, 6st 7lbs (Osborne).

Betting—4 to 1 Chicago, 6 to 1 Carlyon, 7 to 1 Whakawai, 8 to 1 Mentor or Tradition, 12 to 1 Ensign, Australian Peer, Bravo or The Yeoman. 20 to 1 Arsenal, Malua, Dick Swiveller, Cyclops or Spade Guinea, 30 to 50 to 1 others.

Lord Headington was first away and led across the tan, followed by Malua, Mentor, Ensign, Bravo, Tradition and Whakawai. Melos, however, was in front by the time the course proper was reached, and led gaily past the stand at a rattling pace, followed by Spade Guinea, Newmaster, Menotti, Bravo and Malua in a bunch. Then came Tradition, Australian Peer, Arsenal and Ilex almost in a line, while Meteor, E.D. and Recall were last. Round the turn and down the river side Melos still led, but was joined by Malua before the bridge was reached. Australian Peer and Mentor also improved their positions, while Spade Guinea broke down. Passing the bridge the order was Malua, Melos and Mentor, while in close attendance were Dick Swiveller, Whakawai, Australian Peer and Newmaster in a line. Ilex's colours suddenly flashed in front along the back stretch, but in a few strides Cyclops was in the van, and led past the abattoirs three lengths from Whakawai and Bravo with Mentor close by. At the distance post The Yeoman was on terms with Cyclops, Bravo and Whakawai being next ; then came Mentor and Tradition, both of whom shot forward at the half distance. Mentor took the lead, and, although challenged by Tradition, won by half a length, The Yeoman being a good third just in front of Cyclops.

Time—3min. 30¾secs.

FRANCIS LONGMORE'S "TIP!"

For years past F. Longmore and Co. have been justly celebrated for the excellence of their Veterinary Medicines and proprietary articles—a fact acknowledged by all racing men and owners of horses. Scarcely a stable of any importance or standing will be found without some of our specialities, which past experience has proved to be invariably reliable and effective. This fact will be easily understood and appreciated when we remind our clients that the particular department devoted to the manufacture of Veterinary Medicines is conducted by a gentleman possessing the requisite knowledge, skill and long experience indispensable in assuring a perfect method ot manipulation and preparation.

The latest addition to our **Veterinary List** is

LONGMORE'S RED BLISTER
FOR HORSES,

As the safest and best remedy for **Curbs, Splints, Spavins, Sore Shins, or Thickening of the Tendons of the Horse.**

The chief features of the Blister are as follows:—Briskness in Action, Absolute Certainty in Result, and Minimum of Pain to the Horse. It never leaves a blemish, and the animal can be turned loose or worked without hindrance, as it will not gnaw the parts. The hair always grows again in ten days. Since the Blister was first introduced, it has stood the severest tests by men of undoubted ability and experience, to whom a personal reference is permitted. By them it is accepted as a remedy of the highest merit—the right thing for every racing stable in the colony; and we therefore confidently recommend it to the notice of the sporting world.

Full Directions and Testimonials with each Pot.

The Red Blister is sold in Pots at 2s. 6d., 4s. 6d. and 10s. 6d. each.

One Sample Pot will be sent Free on receipt of 2s. 6d. in stamps to any Owner or Trainer in the Colony.

Can be obtained direct from the Manufacturer or any respectable Chemist. **Take no other.**

ADDRESS—

FRANCIS LONGMORE & CO.,
Mercantile Pharmacies,

183 BOURKE ST.; 490, 504 FLINDERS ST., MELBOURNE;
141 BRUNSWICK STREET, NORTH FITZROY;
And Canterbury Road, Surrey Hills.

Trained by W. Higginbotham.   M.ENTOR, 1888.   Ridden by Mick O'Brien.
Hon: D.S. Wallace.

Of the twenty-eight Cup races that have been contested, thirteen have been won by representatives of New South Wales, while Victoria has asserted her protective policy to the extent of appropriating the same number to herself. Of the remaining two, one fell to the lot of South Australia, and Tasmania carried off the other.

Though the New Zealanders have not yet taken the coveted prize to their shores, they have still been successful in furnishing a winner, but in this respect New South Wales bears the palm, ten winners having been bred in the mother colony, while Victoria scores nine. Of the rest Tasmania has produced four and South Australia three.

Something like £50,000 in prize money has been expended up to date, and of this amount Victoria managed to retain nearly £25,000. Considerably over £20,000 went to New South Wales, while Tasmania and South Australia divided the balance pretty nearly equally between them. The smallest stake (£510) was in 1863 (Banker's year), and the highest prize (£4885) in 1888 (Mentor's year). Of the latter, however, £600 went to the second horse and £300 to the third.

TELEPHONE 1125. **Spring Carts for Hire.**

F. C. EASTWOOD,

Wholesale ♣ Bottle ♣ Merchant,

NOS. 130, 132, 134, 136 RAE-ST., NORTH FITZROY,

AND

27, 29, 31, 33 SEACOMBE STREET, MELBOURNE.

F. C. E. begs to notify to persons dealing in the country that he receives all descriptions of Marine Stores at the railway stations or wharves, pays freight, and returns cash for same every Saturday. Having been 16 years in Fitzroy, and being in a position to give a fair market price, consignees may depend on being dealt with liberally.

Feference—English, Scottish and Australian Chartered Bank.

Robert Mitchell

Begs to inform the

RACING COMMUNITY

That he is still Proprietor of the

Racecourse Hotel,

FLEMINGTON,

WHERE

FIRST-CLASS ACCOMMODATION

Is Provided for Trainers and their Horses.

THE BOXES ARE SPACIOUS AND WELL-VENTILATED.

SUPPLIES OF THE

Best Brands of Beers and Liquors

Are Always on Hand, while the

ACCOMMODATION IS COMFORTABLE and HOMELY.

Owners requiring accommodation for the Spring Racing Season are requested to make early application.

Parties wanting Boxes at any time can have them retained per receipt of Telegram.

As the Hotel is situated close to the Course, Trainers will find it Most Convenient.

SCOTT AND YOUNG,

Patentees and Sole Manufacturers of the

ALTHOUSE WINDMILL.

The Strongest, Simplest, Most Durable, and Best Self-Regulating Windmill in the Market.

Proved by Actual Experience to be Unequalled for Water Supply Purposes.

FOUR SIZES—10ft., 12ft., 14ft., and 16ft.—Kept in Stock.   Larger Sizes Made as Required.

IS ABSOLUTELY THE STRONGEST MILL IN THE MARKET.

Its Extreme Sensitiveness is one of its Greatest Merits.

ITS SELF-REGULATING CAPACITY IS PERFECT.

Guaranteed the Cheapest Mill in the Market.

ATLAS COMPANY OF ENGINEERS,

108, 110, 112, 114 Bouverie Street, Carlton, Melbourne.

The Favourite STOPPING PLACE for Visitors from the
Goulbourn Valley is the

OLD ESTABLISHED

BULL + AND + MOUTH

HOTEL,

BOURKE STREET E., MELBOURNE.

●●●●●●●●●●●●●●●●●●●●●●●●

FIRST-CLASS ACCOMMODATION

For Country and Intercolonial Visitors.

●●●●●●●●●●●●●●●●●●●●●

Smoking, Reading & Billiard Rooms.

LUNCHEON AT ONE P.M.

Night Porter.　　Hot and Cold Baths.

J. D. M'DOUGALL,

Telephone No. 380.　　　　　　　*Proprietor.*

Williams's

AUSTRALIAN

YEAST POWDER.

The Best Article for producing

Light Bread, Tea Cakes & Pastry.

---

*Protected by Royal Letters Patent, and GUARANTEED
absolutely PURE.*

**If you find your Bread, Pastry, &c., heavy and indigestible,
you will find that, by some oversight, some inferior preparation
has been used instead of the genuine WILLIAMS'S; therefore,**

Beware of Worthless Imitations,

And be careful to secure

Williams's.

IN TINS at 6d. the ½lb.

Kruse's Insecticide,

THE

Great Destroyer of Insect Pests.

FOR THE HOUSE,
THE CONSERVATORY,
AND THE GARDEN.

HARMLESS TO ANIMAL LIFE,

And Can be Used with Safety for

CLEANSING - DOMESTIC - PETS.

Preserves Furs from Moth.   Beware of Imitations.

Kruse's

IS THE ONLY ORIGINAL AND ONLY GENUINE.

A Lady writes :—" Life in the Bush would be unendurable but for KRUSE'S Insecticide.

Sold in Tins at 1s. and Upwards.

Wm. S. Husbands

PRACTICAL

OPTICIAN,

454 BOURKE ST. W.

(LATE OF QUEEN STREET),

Has in Stock a Large and Varied Assortment of Spectacles and Eye Glasses, Opera, Field and Marine Glasses.

MATHEMATICAL AND OPTICAL INSTRUMENTS.

Established 1862.   Bristol, England, 1762.

VETERINARY COLLEGE,

BRUNSWICK STREET, FITZROY.

STAFF:

W. T. KENDALL, M.R.C.V.S., PRINCIPAL.

PROF. MCBRIDE, M.R.C.V.S., M.A., Ph.D. | PROF. GOULE, M.R.C.V.S.
DR. J. F. JOYCE, L.R.C.P. | C. J. VYNER, M.R.C.V.S.
PROF. JACKSON, B.Sc., F.C.S.. M.P.S. | S. S. CAMERON, M.R.C.V.S.

Hospital Accommodation for 60 Patients.
606 Cases Admitted for Treatment during 1888.
Practical Instruction Given Daily.

The Curriculum for Veterinary Students extends over a Four Years' Course.

— **Amateur Class for Stock-owners' Sons.** —

PROSPECTUS ON APPLICATION.

CASES IN TOWN AND COUNTRY PROMPTLY ATTENDED

Telephone No. 905.   Specially prepared PLEURO LYMPH supplied.